CREATING
Vintage
Style

CREATING
Vintage
Style

**STYLISH IDEAS
& STEP-BY-STEP
PROJECTS**

LUCINDA GANDERTON

RYLAND
PETERS
& SMALL

LONDON NEW YORK

Senior Designer Megan Smith
Editor Miriam Hyslop
Picture Researcher Emily Westlake
Production Controller Gemma Moules
Art Director Anne-Marie Bulat
Editorial Director Julia Charles
Publishing Director Alison Starling

First published in the United States in 2006
by Ryland Peters & Small, Inc.
519 Broadway
5th Floor
New York, NY 10012
www.rylandpeters.com

Cataloging-in-Publication Data
is available from the Library of
Congress on request.

Printed in China.

10 9 8 7 6 5 4 3 2

ISBN-10: 1 84597 126 4
ISBN-13: 978 1 84597 126 7

contents

introduction

"Contemporary vintage" is at first glance an oxymoron, but this term defines an innovative approach to interior decoration that has transformed the way we think about our homes. Although inspired by the past, it has little to do with recreating an authentic historic look with period paint colors, stenciled walls, and accurate cornicing. It is not a pastiche, but is instead an eclectic, informal way of decorating, sometimes nostalgic but never cloying.

Creating vintage style involves distilling the best elements of previous decades and mixing them with the new, to create a look that is unquestionably modern and which works as well in a country hideaway as it does in an urban apartment. The inspirational interiors featured in this book show just how this can be done throughout the house, from the kitchen and dining room to your study, the children's playroom, and out into the garden. All these rooms are characterized by their effortless blend of old and new furniture, fabrics, accessories, and the finishing touches that make them so individual.

The pleasure in this relaxed lifestyle comes from surrounding yourself with objects that you like and enjoy, irrespective of their age or provenance, so a string of Christmas lights can be hung around an engraved Venetian mirror, a set of French enamel canisters lined up under an original Habitat kitchen clock or a patchwork quilt draped happily over a new chesterfield sofa. The die-hard modernist may baulk at placing a plaid travel rug over the back of an Eileen Gray armchair, but the juxtaposition of iconic style and home comforts can be pleasing and harmonious.

There is a considerable element of imagination and originality involved in interpreting the vintage theme. Personal preferences are important, and no two people will re-work the style in the same way. It is here that an extension of the thrifty spirit of "make do and mend," which was so necessary in less affluent eras, comes in. If you think laterally and look at your favorite possessions—whether they are family heirlooms or junk store finds—with a fresh eye and an open mind, you will discover new and unexpected uses for them:

a lace-trimmed linen sheet can be turned into a window blind, a toast rack doubles up as a letter rack, and a salvaged store sign becomes the main decorative feature in your living room. Fine decorative antiques, glass, and porcelain have always been regarded as an investment purchase, to be cared for accordingly, but there are many more affordable items to be found which are better suited to everyday use. It is better not to buy anything that is obviously in a poor state, such as a table with woodworm or tattered, threadbare curtains, but furniture and fabrics in good condition can be customized to suit your taste.

Local auction houses, flea markets, and reputable second-hand stores are the obvious starting places when setting out on the search for interesting old artefacts, but the really dedicated hunter will venture further afield, to trawl architectural salvage yards, *brocante* markets with imported furniture, fabrics and *objets d'art*, along with the regular vintage textile and interior fairs which are advertised in the specialty press. These may involve an early morning start (experienced dealers always take a flashlight, along with a roomy holdall) and you are

bound to find yourself sifting through piles of dismal old junk, but the reward lies in the unexpected find at the bottom of the box and in recognizing its potential.

If you are not tempted by the lure of the vintage hunt, you do have another option. There are plenty of new interpretations of old products and reproductions of classic items available, that are much easier to find and which have an authentic feel. A list of both large-scale and small, independent suppliers for many of these—including suppliers of familiar domestic items such as wooden scrubbing brushes, ostrich feather dusters, blue-and-white striped kitchen ceramics, and galvanized watering cans—can be found at the back of the book. Most of these companies have their own shopping websites, for the Internet is now truly an international marketplace. eBay and similar sites will offer you the thrill of an auction without even having to leave home, and a few minutes surfing will locate just a few of the many dealers from across the world who offer almost anything you can imagine for sale at the press of a key.

living rooms

A contemporary living room is an informal space for unwinding and entertaining, where family and friends can listen to music, watch films, or play together, surrounded by books, favorite objects, photographs, and paintings. The living rooms of previous eras tended towards the formal and coordinated, but try not to over-design your own vintage-style living space. Take inspiration from the interior itself when planning the room scheme. Any original features—an ornate coving, folding wooden shutters, or a carved marble fireplace—will set the tone for the whole décor, or you could add a new focal point such as an oversized gilt-framed mirror. Choose furniture that is easy to live with rather than grand antiques, and mix comfortable new sofas with odd armchairs. Woolen or patchwork throws and feather-filled cushions will make them even more welcoming.

ABOVE, LEFT AND RIGHT The owners of a highly successful salvage company have put their ideas into practice at home by finding inventive new uses for sixteen crates, a school trunk, and sign from a bicycle shop.

BELOW Dark floorboards, seamless cream-painted woodwork, and a white sofa pull this country living space together, while recessed lighting in the window alcoves will increase the sense of space in the evening.

key elements

Color defines both the style and mood of a room, and a harmonious palette should be the starting point when planning a living space, which is usually the busiest and most multifunctional part of the house. Natural textures and colors—either cool tones like slate and gunmetal or warmer sandstones, wood, and teal—are a good, timeless choice and the palest shades are always easy to live alongside. Subtly nuanced light walls, floors, and furniture create an illusion of space, and also provide a consistent background for other design elements and flashes of bright color or pattern.

Try not to overfill your living room: even if it is comparatively large, there should be plenty of space in which to move about and to accommodate extra chairs when needed. Low-level seating and tables reduce the eyelevel and will make a room seem loftier. If you are going to surround yourself with favorite vintage objects, think of it as an art gallery and position the rest of the furniture so that your treasures are set off to best advantage. Symmetrical arrangements, such as the twin sofas on either side of the fireplace, above, or the carefully placed mirrors, opposite, are always pleasing.

THIS PAGE The cool tones of the walls, sofa, mirrors, and ottoman in this textile designer's living room are balanced with an array of bright cushions and throws that reveals her understanding of pattern and color.

ABOVE The ceiling of this paneled room seems higher than it actually is, because the pattern and color have been concentrated on to the divan and woven rug. The round coffee table and sparsely filled shelves increase the overall sense of space.

ABOVE, CENTER Never be afraid to mix radically diverse styles and clashing patterns from different eras; the effect can sometimes be stunning. These two delicate oriental cushions slouch happily against a bold geometric flowered wallpaper from the 1970s.

ABOVE, RIGHT Two variations on a floral theme: as elegant today as when it was first painted in the early eighteenth century, this beautiful, classic Chinese wallpaper makes a good backdrop for a trio of idiosyncratic flowerpot handbags.

BELOW, RIGHT A subtle blend of old and new linked by a predominantly monochrome scheme: the delicate organic print of the contemporary paper complements the glass vases and funky model Eiffel tower, which seem to float against the wall on a clear Perspex table.

Although antique, the Victorian mahogany pieces known in the trade as "brown furniture" are currently out of favor, while mid-twentieth-century design classics, French armoires and dressers, leather sofas, simple shelving, and battered junkshop and flea market finds are finding favor in the most relaxed and convivial rooms. These newer (and usually cheaper) pieces mix well with huge sofas and squashy armchairs to great affect.

All fashions go in cycles, and the style virtues of patterned wallpapers are currently being rediscovered. This time around, they are to be used with discretion: a single wall or a separate panel of wall rather than the in-your-face 1970s visual assault. Retro abstract designs have been reissued, as have historic prints that date back to the early eighteenth century and which would look at home in a stately mansion. Swirly carpets, on the other hand, have yet to be revived, and with good reason. White-painted or polished pine floorboards, sisal matting, and textured carpets are far less dominating within a room scheme, and floor-level pattern now comes from rugs rather than wall-to-wall patterned carpeting.

fabrics

Vintage furnishing textiles, from folk-art patchwork quilts and cotton lace curtains to 1960s op-art roller blinds have survived in great quantities and take on a new lease of life in a contemporary living space. Some are fragile and may need to be mounted carefully as wall hangings and kept away from direct sunlight, but others, such as robust 1950s cottons, will still withstand daily use and regular washing. Older fabrics are often muted in color and this is part of their attraction, but they were not always so subtle. While William Morris earnestly persevered with traditional organic pigments in the later nineteenth century, chemists were busy producing the first synthetic dyes, in surprisingly vivid hues of purple, acid yellow, cerise, and viridian. These were just as bright as the inks in a 1970s abstract print but they have faded greatly over the decades. Several manufacturers and design groups now produce copies of these washed-out floral designs, which are sought after for vintage-style homes.

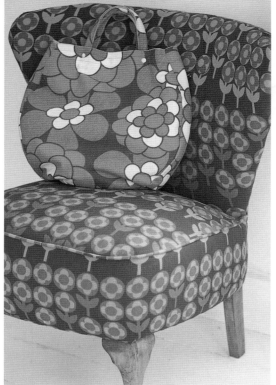

FAR LEFT, BELOW Two panels of narrow striped fabric held down with rows of brass upholstery nails are all the decoration needed on this sturdy chair.

FAR LEFT, ABOVE A row of plump, graphic cushions on a plain upholstered sofa prevent an all-white room from appearing too stark and austere.

ABOVE, LEFT These square mattress-style pads can also be used as floor cushions.

ABOVE, CENTER Back to the decade that style forgot: 1970s prints are now highly desirable.

ABOVE, RIGHT Red, white, and blue flags and cushions, adorned with simple circles of seed pearls, lend a stately air to an old armchair.

LEFT This magnificent hand-embroidered antique silk hanging, as striking as a painting, is mounted on a wooden batten so that the fabric is not put under strain.

LEFT Luscious velvet pansies add the final touch to these kitsch, flowery cushion covers.
FAR LEFT New image transfer techniques mean seaside snaps no longer need to be consigned to an album (see the project on page 22 for a similar cushion).
ABOVE, LEFT A pretty patchwork, a flowery quilt, and a pile of cushions effectively disguise an old sofa.
ABOVE, RIGHT Dress up a plain cushion with a knitted top and a few appliquéd flowers.

When selecting a pattern, remember that large-scale patterns should be used on bigger furniture and tinier designs—use ginghams, ditsy florals, and narrow stripes on smaller pieces, so that the fabric does not engulf the furniture. Light colors or plain fabrics are a good choice for big sofas and armchairs, and will make a room appear spacious. Accents of color and additional texture can then be added with cushions and blankets.

If you prefer a less chintzy, more twentieth-century retro look, there are many later printed fabrics to be found, both originals and reproductions, and you need not limit your search to furnishing fabrics. Interiors are now more relaxed and informal than in the days of piped, frilled cushions and festoon blinds, so be innovative and think of new uses for your old bits and pieces. An interesting silk or cotton scarf can be turned into a square cushion cover with minimal sewing, draped over a lampshade (with a hole cut from the center to prevent scorching), hung up at a window, or used to tie back a curtain. Large throws or dustsheets are useful for instantly revamping sofas and chairs with less-than-perfect upholstery. Much cheaper than slipcovers, they can be layered with travel rugs or quilts for a comfortable, laid-back look.

TOP, LEFT Cover a drum lampshade with fabric by sticking it in place with double-sided tape. Trim the edges with fine braid.
TOP, RIGHT Pleated silk shades like these on a Venetian mirrored sconce can be found in thrift stores or yard sales.
ABOVE, LEFT Block out the view by pinning a hemmed panel directly on to a wooden sash frame.
ABOVE, RIGHT An instant window treatment: screw a hook to the side of the frame, tie back the curtain with a scarf, then loop the knot over the hook.

MATERIALS AND EQUIPMENT
iron-on bonding web
sharp pencil
approximately 20 x 40 in.
(50 x 100 cm) thin black leather
old sheet
55 in. (140 cm) square of silk net
sewing kit

ethereal throw

ethereal throw A stunning combination of white net and black leather, this throw has an ethereal quality that is quite unique—the flower and leaf silhouettes seem to float across the surface of the silk. Its creator, textile artist Karen Nicol, works with leading fashion designers and her true understanding of fabrics is revealed in the pairing of such contrasting weights and textures.

1 Enlarge the flower and leaf motifs on page 102 to their full size. These shapes are all reversed and need to remain so at this stage, since you will be attaching them to the back of the leather in step 3.

2 With the paper side facing upwards, trace the outlines of the motifs on to bonding web using a sharp pencil. You will need approximately 50 motifs in total—the arrangement is quite informal so you can select the ones you like best. Cut the shapes out roughly, allowing a border of about ¼ in. (6 mm) around each one.

3 Following the manufacturer's instructions carefully, iron the adhesive side of the bonding web on to the rough side of the leather, fitting the individual shapes together like a jigsaw.

4 Cut out each shape carefully, following the pencil lines. Where a motif has several elements, cut out just around the main outline at this stage.

5 Fold the old sheet in half and lay it out flat on a hard surface: a tiled or wooden floor is ideal. Put the net on top of the sheet and arrange 9–12 motifs, leather side up, in each corner of the net. Group them loosely to form a random pattern.

6 When you are satisfied with the arrangement, cut out the separate pieces of the complex motifs and space them out. Peel off the backing paper from the motifs; then, following the manufacturer's instructions, iron each shape in place using a pressing cloth to protect the surface of the leather.

transfer print cushion

Instead of keeping your old photographs tucked away, you can transfer the images onto fabric and turn them into cushions to keep for yourself, or to give as nostalgic presents. These covers feature my own favorite family black-and-white snapshots and, to complete the vintage look, I made the borders from original 1960s dressmaking material. You can print digital images directly onto transfer paper (from stationers and photographic stores) from a computer, or have your pictures copied at a printers or copying place.

MATERIALS AND EQUIPMENT

old photograph

plain white cotton fabric

plain-colored fabric (to coordinate with the patterned fabric)

matching sewing thread

patterned fabric

two matching buttons (optional)

14 x 18-in. (35 x 45 cm) cushion

sewing kit

sewing machine

Note:
The measurements (left) are for a 6 x 10-in. (15 x 25 cm) picture and a 14 x 18-in. (35 x 45 cm) rectangular cushion; adapt them as necessary to fit the shape and proportions of your own photograph and pad. The seam allowance throughout is ½ in. (1 cm).

CUTTING OUT
from plain-colored fabric:
for the inner border:
two 2 x 6-in. (5 x 15 cm) strips
two 2 x 12-in. (5 x 30 cm) strips
for the outer border:
two 2 x 14-in. (5 x 35 cm) strips
two 2 x 20-in. (5 x 50 cm) strips
for the back:
one 2½ x 16-in. (6 x 40 cm) strip

from patterned fabric:
for the main border:
two 4 x 8-in. (10 x 20 cm) strips
two 4 x 18-in. (10 x 45 cm) strips
for the back:
two 12 x 16-in. (30 x 40 cm) rectangles

1 Transfer your image on to the white cotton fabric and trim it down to 6 x 10 in. (15 x 25 cm).

2 With right sides facing, pin, tack, and machine stitch the short plain-colored inner border strips to the shorter sides of the picture. Carefully press the seams outwards using a pressing cloth so that the iron does not come into contact with the transferred image. Attach the two long inner borders to the long edges of the picture in the same way.

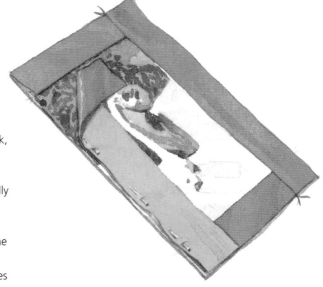

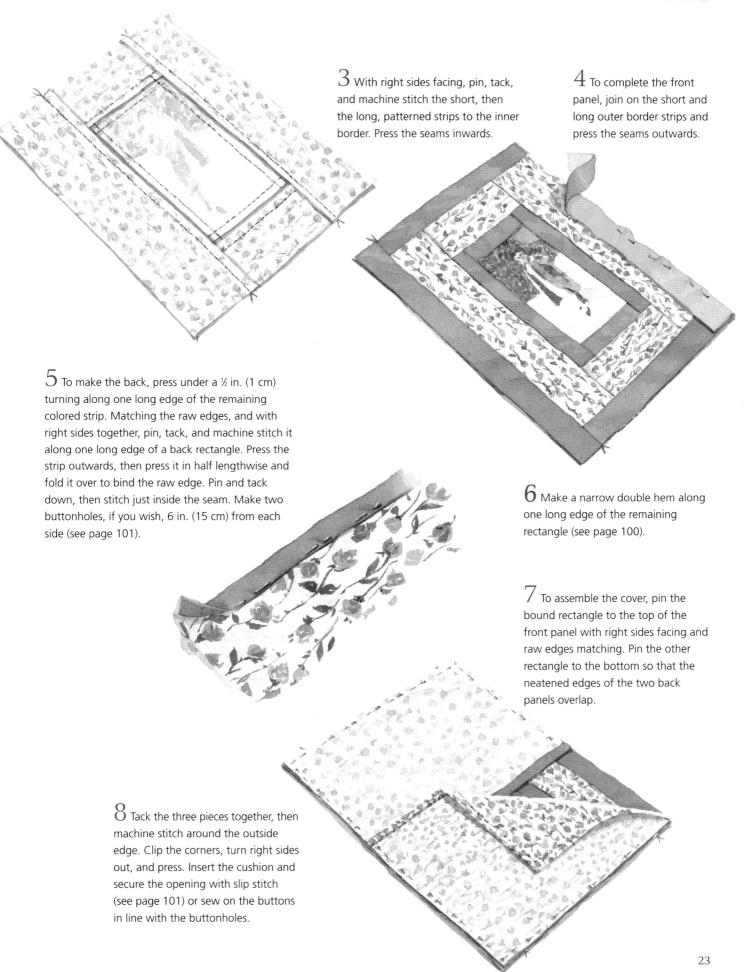

3 With right sides facing, pin, tack, and machine stitch the short, then the long, patterned strips to the inner border. Press the seams inwards.

4 To complete the front panel, join on the short and long outer border strips and press the seams outwards.

5 To make the back, press under a ½ in. (1 cm) turning along one long edge of the remaining colored strip. Matching the raw edges, and with right sides together, pin, tack, and machine stitch it along one long edge of a back rectangle. Press the strip outwards, then press it in half lengthwise and fold it over to bind the raw edge. Pin and tack down, then stitch just inside the seam. Make two buttonholes, if you wish, 6 in. (15 cm) from each side (see page 101).

6 Make a narrow double hem along one long edge of the remaining rectangle (see page 100).

7 To assemble the cover, pin the bound rectangle to the top of the front panel with right sides facing and raw edges matching. Pin the other rectangle to the bottom so that the neatened edges of the two back panels overlap.

8 Tack the three pieces together, then machine stitch around the outside edge. Clip the corners, turn right sides out, and press. Insert the cushion and secure the opening with slip stitch (see page 101) or sew on the buttons in line with the buttonholes.

finishing touches

Once the furniture and soft furnishings have been selected, it may seem that a room scheme is fixed forever, but there are many ways in which you can change the smaller elements in order to alter the ambience and appearance of your living space. One of the most effective ways of doing this is to follow the progress of the seasons throughout the year. Most of us bring in festive decorations at Christmas time, such as the requisite ornamented tree, swags of greenery, candles, and greetings cards. To reinforce this winter change and to create a cosy atmosphere you could also layer your sofa with snug throws, plaid wool blankets, and extra cushions, or add a vintage chenille cloth to your table.

The warmer months, however, require a lighter touch. Spring is the time to bring the outdoors into your living space, with potted plants and vibrant fresh blooms or still-life paintings of flowers and foliage. It is easy to increase the sense of space with pale colors and unfussy fabrics: monogrammed vintage sheets can be hung at the window to diffuse the dappled sunshine or to provide instant camouflage for an old table or chair. Even something as obvious as just putting things away will change the mood.

A well-displayed collection will enhance a room, as long as it is in keeping with the overall style, but care has to be taken to prevent it looking like cluttered bric-a-brac.

OPPOSITE Metal furniture looks just as good indoors as it does in the garden, either in a conservatory or in the corner of a living room.

ABOVE, LEFT As an alternative to hanging paintings on the wall, an artist's easel can be used to display old unframed canvases, instead of the usual work in progress.

ABOVE, RIGHT Two rows of clear glass containers, each holding a single stem, have much greater visual impact than a single vase of flowers.

CENTER, RIGHT The stalks of these roses have been cut short so that the heads mass together, forming a dome of color like the lid of the teapot.

CENTER, LEFT, AND BELOW, LEFT Narcissus and hyacinth flowers can be forced to bloom early, providing you with a burst of unexpected color in the late winter. Place a layer of moist bulb compost in a shallow bowl, teacup, or dish. Sit the bulbs on the surface so the bottom third is covered, making sure that they do not touch each other. Keep the container in a dark, cool place, watering occasionally, until the first shoots appear, then bring them out to be enjoyed.

BELOW, RIGHT Florists store their bouquets in these galvanized buckets: brighten them up with sheets of colorful paper.

ABOVE AND RIGHT These snapshots and postcards are fixed to the wall with putty adhesive.

TOP, LEFT Perched on the end of a mantelpiece, this exquisite empty frame does not need a picture.

TOP, CENTER Original Venetian frames are now collectors' items but there are many more affordable reproductions around.

TOP, RIGHT A Victorian miniature easel shows off a precious keepsake.

If you are a magpie-like hoarder, it is worth remembering that museums only ever exhibit a small part of their holdings. By rotating and rearranging your own displays, or just putting out a few items at a time, you will show them off to best advantage. A single object on a shelf can look striking, or try grouping items together by shape or color, so that they create their own rhythm and visual patterns. The postcard collage opposite is a good example of this approach.

It is the tiny details that really stamp an owner's personality on a room and make it unique—and this includes the fixtures and fittings, just as much as the contents. For a truly vintage look, you could go as far as replacing modern light switches with reproduction brass or Bakelite toggle switches and changing the door knobs to old china knobs or escutcheons.

27

kitchens & dining rooms

For generations, the kitchen has been the inevitable gathering place for every household; a place where news is exchanged and meals enjoyed by family and visitors alike. Full of activity and at the hub of domestic routine, kitchens are packed with colorful crockery, gadgets, and cooking utensils. It is this functional element that lends kitchen styles from all eras a timeless appeal, which bypasses fashionable trends: a few well-chosen vintage accessories will give a comfortable, lived-in feel to even the most streamlined room. Food preparation and eating together are now part of everyday activity and most contemporary kitchens include space for a breakfast bar, if not a table and chairs. If you have the luxury of a separate dining room, this can provide the perfect setting for both formal and informal entertaining, from gourmet dinners to leisurely weekend lunches.

ABOVE Plain blue linen napkins, folded into simple triangles, lend a bright, café-like air to this chrome breakfast table and matching benches.

BELOW Wall-mounted shelves and freestanding drawers look less formal than built-in cupboards and provide plenty of display space.

key elements

All kitchens are designed around three essential features—sink, refrigerator, and stove—cupboards and shelves for food, pots, and pans. In the past, a pantry and utility room gave additional space for storage and laundry, but if you are planning a kitchen from scratch and wish to create a vintage look, many of the large appliances can be concealed behind cupboard doors and special units. There are, however, alternatives to a fully fitted kitchen. An Aga or range will immediately give period flavor and you can seek out retro-style fridges and washing machines in bright colors or brushed steel. Reproduction or recycled ceramic sinks (the deep ones are called "Belfast" sinks; the shallow ones are "Butler's") can be complemented with old-fashioned faucets and a wooden draining board. Refurbish kitchen furniture from auctions or salvage yards: enamel-topped tables or butcher's blocks provide useful work surfaces. The traditional dresser with its tiered shelving was originally intended for daily use, but also as a showcase for ornamental pitchers, meat dishes, and the best tea set.

OPPOSITE, RIGHT This fine antique mahogany dining table was once accompanied by a set of six matching chairs. Proving that new vintage style is far from a slavish period recreation, the owner has surrounded the table with an unexpected selection of chairs: a utility seat, two Victorian Thonet bentwoods, and a woven cane chair from the mid-twentieth century.

THIS PAGE In another example of how effective mismatched seating can look, these four assorted spindle-backed kitchen chairs have been painted in toning pale pastel shades. The walls, plate rack, baseboards, and floorboards are all white, which gives the room a spacious, airy feeling, and the only bright color comes from the floral ceramic dishes.

LEFT This scalloped machine-embroidered French shelf trim was a flea market find. Create a similar look with a piece of crochet edging.

fabrics

Kitchen textiles, from ticking aprons and shelf edgings to pictorial dishtowels, have an air of cosy familiarity about them. Genuinely old accessories, and those made from new fabric in vintage-style prints, can be used to soften gleaming expanses of tiled or granite surfaces and add individuality to the heart of the home. A couple of generations ago, no kitchen was complete without a handy array of clothespin bags, potholders, tea cosies, and embroidered tray cloths. These items more or less disappeared during the minimalist late twentieth century, but they are now making a welcome comeback. They are not just nostalgic, but also practical: clean, old linen drying cloths, for example, can be put to daily use and are still the best way to dry fine glassware.

Antique table linen, both plain and embroidered, is plentiful and easy to find: even if you cannot locate a complete set, a damask cloth and eight non-matching white napkins can look striking, particularly if they all have different edgings or initials. The fabric can be revived by washing at a high temperature and pressing with a hot iron whilse slightly damp. Spray-on starch or silicon stiffener will restore a clean, crisp finish. Elsewhere in the kitchen, vintage curtains can be laundered, ironed, and altered to fit your own windows, to keep drafts away from the back door, or fitted on sprung wire under draining boards and work surfaces.

OPPOSITE, ABOVE RIGHT Checkered fabrics always look bright and cheerful.

OPPOSITE, BELOW Hide your modern appliances behind a 1950s curtain.

ABOVE To make a runner, cut a long rectangle, half the width of the table, and allow a 4-in. (10 cm) overhang at each end. Hem all around and trim with toning tassels, braid and a pleated frill.

ABOVE, CENTER Store matching napkins in sets by tying them together with braid or ribbon.

ABOVE, RIGHT This handle cover is made from two pieces of felted wool.

RIGHT Oilcloth and plastic-coated tablecloths are practical, yet stylish.

BELOW, RIGHT Cutlery rolls are ideal for picnics.

BELOW, CENTER Make this holder by pressing the corners of a napkin to the center. Sew three sides together and sew a fastener to the fourth.

BELOW, LEFT These monogrammed napkins were once an essential part of a girl's trousseau.

apron Even a novice cook will be transformed into an accomplished domestic goddess by this retro-style reversible apron. Designer Emily Medley has used two bold geometric prints, in a characteristic 1970s yellow, orange, and brown color scheme, and both sides have a large and practical pocket. Only basic sewing skills are needed to put it all together and the effect is stunning.

MATERIALS AND EQUIPMENT
main cotton fabric
contrasting cotton fabric
matching sewing thread
sewing machine
sewing kit

CUTTING OUT
apron
For the front, cut a 33 x 40-in. (85 x 100 cm) rectangle from the main fabric. Fold in half, long edges together, with right sides facing. Pin together along the top and half of the side edges. Mark a point on the top 11 in. (28 cm) in from the corners and a second point on the sides 12 in. (30 cm) down. Draw a curve to join the points. Pin just inside the line, then cut along it. Cut the back to the same size from the contrasting fabric.

from the contrasting print cut:
tabs: two 1½ x 6 in. (4 x 15 cm) strips
ties: two 2½ x 36 in. (6 x 92 cm) strips
neck loop: 2½ x 24 in. (6 x 60 cm) strip
appliqué: Cut out two life-sized wooden-spoon shapes from the contrasting print.

pockets
From the main fabric, cut a 10 x 20 in. (25 x 50 cm) rectangle. Fold in half, short edges together, and draw a curve across one corner. Pin both layers together just inside the curve, then cut out. Cut another pocket from the contrasting fabric to the same shape.

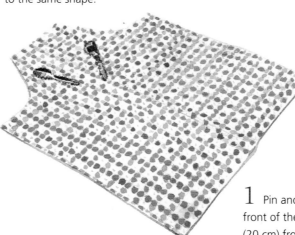

1 Pin and tack the two "spoons" to the front of the apron, one on each side, 8 in. (20 cm) from the top. Set the machine to a zigzag stitch and sew around the edges.

2 Fold under and press a ⅔ in. (2 cm) double hem along the top of each pocket. Machine stitch close to the inner fold. Cut small notches along the curves, then press under ⅔ in. (2 cm) around the raw edges.

3 To make the tabs, press each strip in half, long sides together, with wrong sides facing, then press a ½-in (1 cm) turning along each long edge and refold. Pin and tack the edges together, then work a row of machine stitch ⅛-in. (3 mm) in from each side.

4 Fold one tab into a loop and tack to the wrong side of the pocket, 6 in. (15 cm) from the right corner. Do the same with the second tab on the other pocket.

5 Pin and tack the first pocket to the front, covering the ends of the spoons, and machine stitch close to the edge. Work a second line of stitches ½ in. (1 cm) further in. Sew the second pocket to the back in the same way.

6 Make up the neck loop and ties as for the tabs, pressing under one short end of each tie to neaten. Pin and tack the neck loop to the right side of the front, ½ in. (1 cm) in from the top corners, raw edges together. Pin and tack the open ends of the ties in place on the side edges, ½ in. (1 cm) down from the bottom of the curve, raw edges together.

7 With right sides facing and the neck loop and ties drawn into the middle, pin and tack the front and back together, leaving the bottom edge open. Clip the corners, then turn right side out and press. Press under a ¾-in. (2 cm) hem around the open edge, then pin, tack, and machine stitch the edge together.

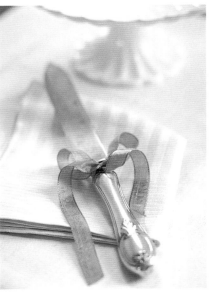

finishing touches

ABOVE, LEFT These quirky egg cosies are made from quarter-circles cut from densely felted wool and stitched into cones.

ABOVE, CENTER White table linen and classic cutlery are a timeless combination; add an elegant touch by tying a ribbon bow around a silver cake knife.

ABOVE, RIGHT Look out for old milk bottles, especially those printed with advertising slogans or the name of a dairy.

RIGHT No afternoon tea tray is complete without a crochet pitcher cover; make your own by sewing glass beads around the border of a dainty lace mat.

LEFT A fluted cup from grandmother's best tea set makes the perfect container for a single old-fashioned bloom, like this subtle-hued anemone.

OPPOSITE A varied assortment of 1970s tins shares a characteristically vivid color scheme.

Along with treasured pottery, glassware, and canteens of cutlery, many old kitchen utensils still survive after decades of continued use. Scales with brass weights, hand-turned coffee grinders, and loaf pans can be found at antique markets or specialty dealers, and there is great pleasure to be had in putting them to their original purpose (if they are clean and still in good condition). They can otherwise simply be collected as decorative objects and grouped by color, type, or pattern.

Old white ceramic jello molds, storage containers with stenciled lettering, and pressed-glass cake stands are far more ornamental than their modern counter-parts, but if you cannot locate the originals there are some kitchen classics that are still in production. English pottery firm T. G. Green and Co. has manufactured its signature blue-and-white striped Cornish Ware in the Midlands since the 1920s, and, nearby at Church Gresley, Mason Cash still create traditional embossed mixing bowls from the local clay. Other items remain unchanged: a new wooden spoon, lemon squeezer, or balloon whisk is more or less indistinguishable from one that was made 50 years ago. Some, more ephemeral, objects were not intended to last for a long time and survive only by default.

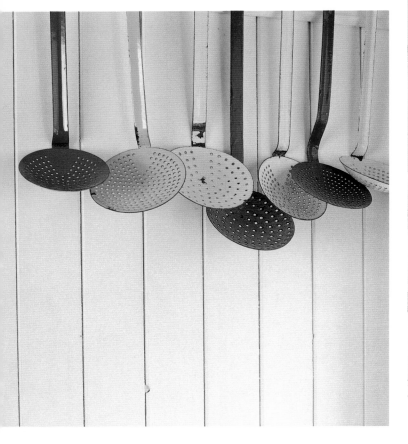

ABOVE, LEFT Old enamel strainers, in a range of subtly muted colors, make an effective display. **ABOVE, RIGHT** This carefully selected assortment of nineteenth-century

French enamel kitchenware is both decorative and practical. **BELOW** A row of vintage postcards enlivens the dreary task of washing up: protect them with a piece of glass or Plexiglass.

Stoneware jars, commemorative tins, and canisters, or molded glass bottles, are now much sought after. They look very effective displayed alongside new, inexpensive collectibles: colorful food packaging from Thai or Chinese supermarkets, interesting sardine or soda cans, or flower-painted Thermos flasks.

When it comes to kitchen china, the days of the vast dinner service, complete with three sizes of plates, several tureens, and oval serving dishes, are long gone: few of us have the space to store so much crockery and entertaining is far less formal. You can, however, make a special mealtime seem unique with a few well-chosen details. Napkin rings, a small posy of flowers, or a bow on the stem of a glass will all make a place setting seem special. Matching tea sets were also once commonplace but you can create a new twist on the theme by hanging your odd cups on hooks under shelves or units. Afternoon tea itself is a relaxing social event that is ripe for revival: a tray arranged with a dainty embroidered cloth, a pitcher of milk, a china teapot, and a bowl of sugar lumps—whether coordinated or not—has its own particular charm.

LEFT Prettily decorated cups and saucers are evocative of more sedate days: collect a mismatched set and invite your friends around for tea and cakes.

BELOW, RIGHT Tie a spray of lily of the valley with organza ribbon and lay it across a wine glass as an individual favor.

BELOW, CENTER A pink hydrangea head has been fixed to the back of this chair with a loosely tied ribbon bow—a personal touch for a special party.

BELOW, LEFT Sometimes the smallest details can be the most effective: the fluted border of the dinner plate echoes the simple bead trim on these brown linen napkins.

heart of fresh roses

Set the scene for a special lunch or dinner party with this romantic garland, designed by Paula Pryke. A heart-shaped foam base makes the perfect framework for a delicate display of fragrant pink "Anna" roses, palest green guelder roses and, lacy white hydrangeas, which can be used as a table centerpiece or hung from the dining-room wall.

MATERIALS AND EQUIPMENT

heart-shaped floral foam base,
17 in. (43 cm) across at widest point

20 in. (50 cm) green velvet ribbon,
1½ in. (3.5 cm) wide (optional)

30 pink roses (*Rosa* "Anna")

27 sprigs guelder rose
(*Viburnum opulus*)

6 white hydrangeas
(*Hydrangea macrophylla*)

florist's knife

heavy-gauge stub wire

florist's scissors

1 Soak the heart-shaped foam base in water for five minutes. Then, using a florist's knife, trim away a strip of foam about 1 in. (2.5 cm) wide on both the inner and outer edges. This will make the base more three-dimensional.

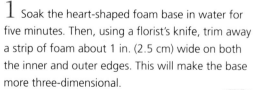

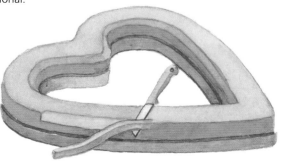

2 If you plan to hang the garland, tie the velvet ribbon around the top of the foam base with a double knot. To prevent it from slipping, bend a stub wire into a U-shape and push it into the foam so that it straddles the ribbon and pins it in place.

3 Using florist's scissors, trim the stems of the roses to within 2 in. (5 cm) of the rose heads. Arrange the roses around the heart shape, inserting the stems so that the flowers face to the right and left of the base.

4 When you have laid the foundation of pink roses, fill in the heart with guelder roses. Cut down the stems to 2 in. (5 cm) and insert the green florets of guelder rose around the roses on the inner and outer edges.

5 Divide each hydrangea flower into two or three groups of florets. Finish off the display by filling in any remaining exposed areas of foam on the heart shape with small groups of these delicate white flowers.

bedrooms

Whether you long for a flower-strewn boudoir, fantasize about the fifties chic of a glamour puss, or simply yearn for a comfortable retreat at the end of the day, your bedroom is the one place where you can truly express your individual style within your own personal space. We spend up to a third of our day in our bedrooms and, although much of that time is passed sleeping, it is important to create a tranquil ambience for cosseting, romance, and rest alike. A vintage-themed décor, with its seamless combination of old and new, will give you the best of all worlds, whatever the age and style of your home. Succumb to your inner nesting instinct and surround yourself with the home comforts of a previous era: patchwork quilts, paisley comforters, bolsters, and old-fashioned counterpanes, but don't stint when it comes to hunting down suitable new downy feather pillows and a bouncy, well-sprung mattress to accompany them.

key elements

A serene atmosphere is conducive to peaceful sleep, so aim to create a calm mood in your bedroom. Too much color and pattern can prove overwhelming, but by starting out with a neutral background of pale walls, floors, and ceiling, you can add an assortment of curtains, rugs, and accessories without the overall look becoming too cluttered. Remember that built-in closets take up less space than freestanding wardrobes, and look out for old vanity, cheval, or wall mirrors, which will add an airy feeling by reflecting light back into the room.

The bed is, inevitably, the most dominant feature, but careful choice of linen and covers will reduce the visual impact. Old wooden and metal bedsteads are characterful, but were not designed for modern comfort. Check the springing or base slats before buying and make sure you get a supportive new mattress. There are also many reproduction beds on the market, which are wider than the originals. New paint will soften the look of dark-colored wooden bedsteads and other old furniture and turn junk-store finds into one-of-a-kind pieces. Strip the wax or existing paint from old pine washstands, wardrobes and dressing tables, and repaint with one of the many shades of off-white paint.

ABOVE, LEFT Original or period French armoires are perfect for storing clothes. To keep out dust and moths, remove any wire panels and replace them with safety glass. Staple a piece of fabric—either plain or with a bold pattern—inside the frame to conceal the contents. The floral chintz used here complements perfectly the monochrome Toile de Jouy cherub print on the adjacent full-length curtains perfectly.

BELOW, LEFT Once the place where a 1920s flapper completed her toilette, this wooden dressing table with its long oval mirror and useful drawers has been given a fresher, more contemporary look with a coat of off-white paint in a satin finish. An embroidered pashmina, chosen to harmonize with the lush flowered curtains, has been thrown over the padded stool as a more relaxed alternative to an upholstered seat.

LEFT In an undeniably contemporary setting, an old quilted bedspread effectively softens the industrial lines of a steel bed frame.

MAIN PICTURE Expanses of plain white paintwork give this bedroom a light and airy feel, and provide an understated backdrop for the eclectic accessories.

voile bed canopy

The elegant cascades of this Regency-style flowery drape, from leading soft furnishings expert Katrin Cargill, lend an air of romance to a classic bedroom. Although the effect is dramatic, it is surprisingly easy to put together from a length of floaty voile gathered onto a short curtain rod, then attached to the wall with a bracket.

MATERIALS AND EQUIPMENT

floral voile fabric

plain cotton fabric for lining

short wooden curtain rod
with bracket and finial

sewing machine

sewing kit

1 Center the bracket above the bed and fix it securely to the wall with long screws. Measure the distance from the top of the bracket to the floor. Add 1 yd (1 m) to this measurement, plus 8 in. (20 cm) for the hem. Double this figure for your final length of fabric: a single furnishing width will be sufficient.

2 Cut the voile in half across the width. With right sides facing and the pattern running in the same direction on each panel, pin and tack the two top edges together with a ⅔ in. (2 cm) seam. Press open.

3 Cut the cotton lining to the same length as the uncut voile. Fold it in half across the width and press the fold.

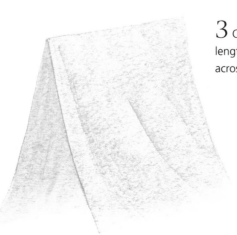

4 Press under a double ½ in. (1 cm) hem (see page 100) along the long edges of the voile, then press under a double 1½ in. (4 cm) turning along the short edges. Miter the corners (see page 101), then pin, tack, and machine stitch the hem around all four edges.

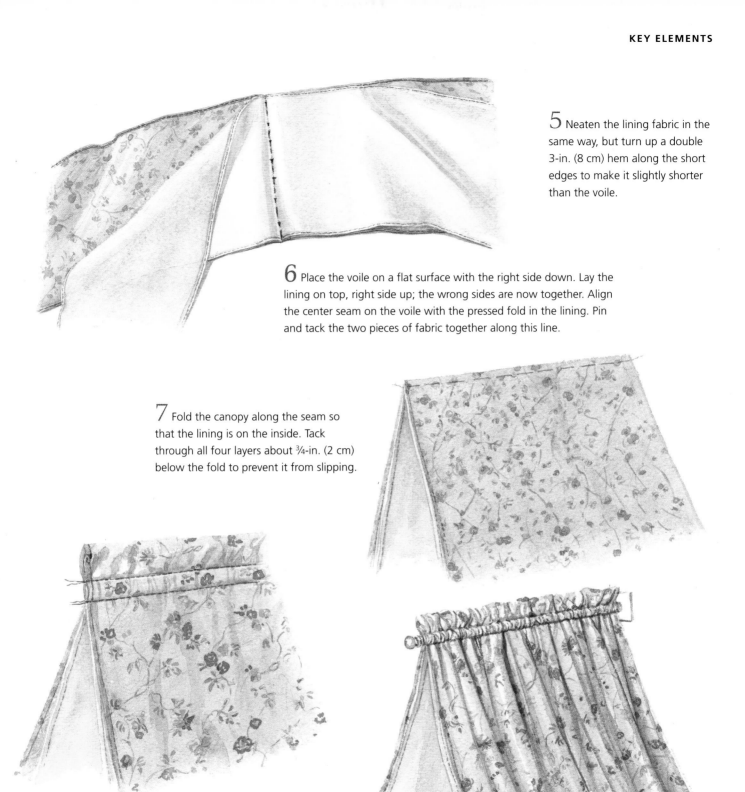

5 Neaten the lining fabric in the same way, but turn up a double 3-in. (8 cm) hem along the short edges to make it slightly shorter than the voile.

6 Place the voile on a flat surface with the right side down. Lay the lining on top, right side up; the wrong sides are now together. Align the center seam on the voile with the pressed fold in the lining. Pin and tack the two pieces of fabric together along this line.

7 Fold the canopy along the seam so that the lining is on the inside. Tack through all four layers about ¾-in. (2 cm) below the fold to prevent it from slipping.

8 Using a dressmaker's pen, mark two parallel lines for the casing across the width of the canopy. The first should be 2 in. (5 cm) below the fold and the second a further 1¼ in. (3 cm) beneath that. Pin and tack along the lines and check that the rod fits into the casing. Adjust the position of the second line if necessary, then machine stitch along both lines.

9 Insert the rod into the casing and adjust the ruffles evenly. Slot the finial onto the rod, and then screw the other end into the bracket.

fabrics

FAR LEFT This well-worn but much-loved Victorian patchwork is made entirely from silk diamonds embellished with hand embroidery.
LEFT To make a scented lavender or rose sachet, sew two rectangles of fabric together around three sides, turn right side out and fill with a handful of dried flowers. Slip stitch the fourth edge closed, then bind with ribbon.
BOTTOM AND BELOW, LEFT AND RIGHT Use bows of satin or organza ribbon to add a feminine touch to blankets, curtains, and cushions.

RIGHT Turn an unused alcove into storage space by hanging floral curtains from a rail fixed at ceiling height. Keep them drawn back to showcase a pretty summer dress within.
FAR RIGHT Sew scraps of old lace and cutwork mats onto small cushions, then fill with potpourri so they release their fragrance when moved.
RIGHT, BELOW This stack of assorted vintage quilts shows how different patterns will merge together when they share a common color scheme.

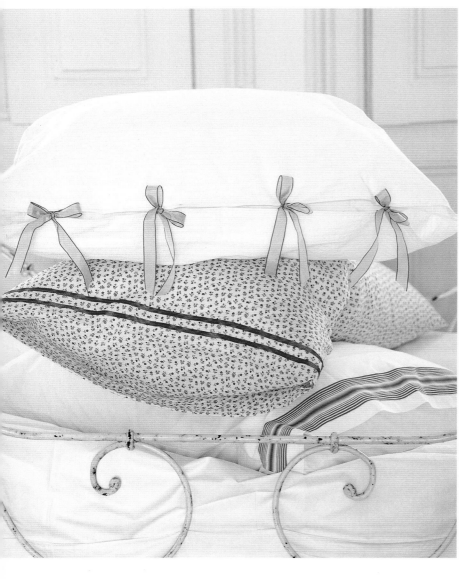

As the bedroom's largest piece of furniture and main focal point, your bed provides the ideal background for showing off an assortment of interesting textile pieces. Layered accessories always give a more stylish look than a single large cover, so display neatly folded antique quilts, brightly colored crocheted afghans, or a pile of flowery cushions against basic white sheets and pillowcases. This is a quick way to transform the look of your bedroom, and one which you can easily change to match the seasons—cuddle up to fluffy woolen blankets and satin comforters during the winter and keep cool in the warmer months with Egyptian cotton sheets and a mosquito net or draped voile canopy. If you have an attractive old-style wrought-iron or brass bedstead, make the most of it by hanging simple fabric bags for nighttime necessities from the frame. On the other hand, a bulky divan base can be played down with a fitted white cotton valance and a sheet or cotton throw draped over a padded headboard.

Antique bedlinen, especially that from France and Eastern Europe, has become highly sought after in recent years and specialty dealers now import these fabrics in bulk. Old hemp or pure linen sheets and pillowcases have an unmistakable feel that only comes from decades of washing and

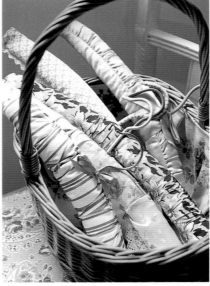

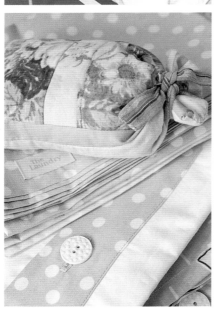

ironing, and often feature beautifully embroidered monograms dating from their days as part of a young bride's trousseau. Look out also for inside edging featuring hand-stitched mottoes or lace, along with delicate openwork or hemstitching trims—or add your own to plain linen. Undersized or damaged sheets can be cut down and reused as cushion or pillow covers or incorporated into patchwork designs. Remember that even the smallest scraps and remnants can be used to cover padded coat hangers or pieced together to make drawstring bags in which to store everything from the laundry to cosmetics.

Although down-filled comforters and blankets have long been superseded by the more practical comforters, the latter are always useful for adding extra warmth and color. Old fringed Welsh rugs, with their muted checkerboard patterns, will sit happily alongside new mohair or plaids. Plain bed blankets are traditionally finished with satin ribbon: stitch a border of narrow ribbon into open-weave wool as a twist on this theme. Elsewhere, cotton tape, braid, and silky ribbons can be tied into bows to make cushion cover closures, curtain tabs, or simply to lend a pretty and slightly frivolous air to an ultra-feminine bedroom.

THIS PICTURE Translucent lacy fabric in pale colors always looks glamorous: these girly bags are trimmed with shiny ribbon bows and antique buckles.

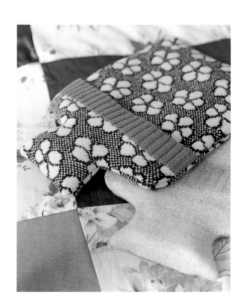

ABOVE Not all your clothes have to be put away: too pretty to hide, this vintage blouse is the perfect complement to the rose-print paper on the wall behind.
RIGHT A collection of interesting patterned handkerchiefs from the mid-twentieth century is displayed on a miniature ladder.
FAR RIGHT Cover your old hot water bottles with knitted woolen fabric recycled from an worn-out cardigan, then snuggle up cosily on a chilly winter night.

MATERIALS AND EQUIPMENT

a selection of old and new fabrics
of similar weight

rotary cutter (optional)

quilter's ruler (optional)

cutting mat (optional)

12-in. (30 cm) square of thick paper
to use as a template

69-in. (175 cm) square of
backing fabric

four 4 x 69-in. (10 x 175 cm) wide
strips of plain fabric for the border

matching sewing thread

sewing machine

sewing kit

diamond patchwork bedcover

The charm of this traditional patchwork quilt lies in the apparent randomness of the fabrics and the interesting variety of colors used by designer Jeanie Blake. One diagonally striped square block is repeated to create a pattern of concentric diamonds. To achieve a similar spontaneous look, try not to be overly-careful or contrived when selecting and arranging your materials.

1 Sort out and press your fabrics, which should all be cotton and of a similar weight. Cut them into narrow strips of between 2 in. (5 cm) and 4 in. (10 cm) wide. A rotary cutter and quilter's ruler, which enable you to cut quickly and accurately, will speed up this process, but are not essential.

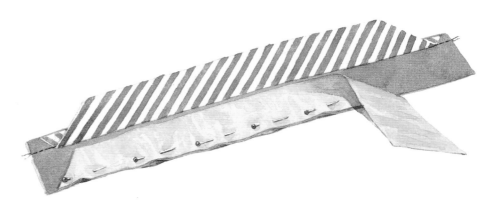

2 Choose a 6 in. (15 cm) strip for the center. Cut a length of different fabric, and trim the ends at 45 degrees. Pin and tack together, then machine stitch with a ¼ in. (6 mm) seam (see page 100). Press the seam outwards. Do the same on the other side, and then add additional strips, each shorter than the last, until you have a square. Check the size against the template as you work.

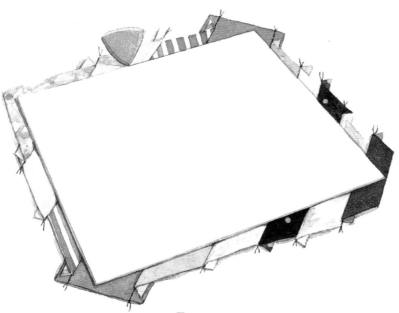

3 Place the template on top of the completed block and draw around it with a dressmaker's pen. Cut out around the line. Make another 35 blocks in the same way, each one different.

4 Lay the blocks out in six rows of six, alternating the direction of the fabric to form an overall diamond design. Take some time arranging them so that you get the best balance of pattern and color within the design.

5 With right sides facing, pin, tack, and machine stitch the first two pairs of blocks together with a ½-in. (1 cm) seam. Press the seams to opposite sides, then join the two pairs to make a large square. Sew the remaining blocks together to make eight more squares, and then join the squares into three rows. Complete by seaming the rows together.

6 Lay the backing fabric on the floor with the right side facing downwards. Place the patchwork centrally on top with the right side upwards and pin together around the outside edge, smoothing the layers from the center to ensure they lie flat. Tack together ½-in. (1 cm) from the edge, then trim away the surplus backing fabric.

7 Press under ½ in. (1 cm) along each side of the four strips of plain border fabric, then press each one in half lengthwise. Fold the first strip over one edge of the quilt and pin, then tack in place. Stitch it down by hand or machine and trim the binding in line with the corners.

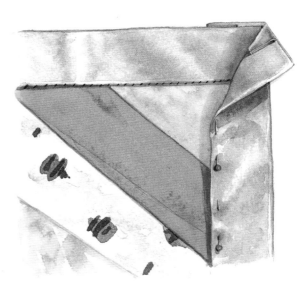

8 Pin a folded strip to the next edge and trim ½ in. (1 cm) from the end adjacent to the first strip. Press the overlap to the wrong side. Tack, then stitch the strip down, and finish off the folded corner with slip stitch (see page 101). Repeat for the other two edges.

finishing touches

ABOVE, LEFT A Florence Nightingale-style concertina night light holder is suspended from the foot of a bedstead.

ABOVE, CENTER The filigree wirework of this tulip-shaped candleholder will cast a delicate lattice of shadows across the windowsill.

ABOVE, RIGHT The flower and leaf-shaped shadows from this old French metal sconce dance and flicker across the wall behind.

RIGHT Billowing, sheer curtains filter the light as it enters your bedroom by day and provide privacy at night. Tie them back with a broad gauzy bow: the black ribbon used here is a pleasing accent that echoes the baroque curves of the furniture.

LEFT A simple shade of softly gathered organza makes a delicate shade for a clear glass lamp.

RIGHT Disparate objects will always harmonize if they have a common theme: hang them on a peg rail against an off-white wall to create the maximum effect.

CENTER, RIGHT Pin a collection of insect and flower brooches to a board instead of keeping them in a jewelry box.

CENTER, LEFT For this informal dressing table, display jewels are simply hung from the neck of translucent glass vases.

BOTTOM, LEFT Enjoy your necklaces all the time by pinning them up.

BOTTOM, RIGHT Victorian ladies displayed their brooches on small padded cushions like this.

It is always pleasing to surround yourself with beautiful objects, and the bedroom is the perfect intimate place to put out all those small collections that would look lost in larger or busier spaces elsewhere in the house. In addition to the china pin dolls, pressed-glass ring stands, perfume atomizers, and swansdown powder puffs that adorned our grandmothers' dressing tables, you are bound to have acquired a host of attractive items that could be displayed. Turn out your cupboards and jewelry boxes in search of handbags, accessories, and strings of pearls or glass beads that you would appreciate looking at every day. Group your treasures according to theme, color, or shape and set them out on delicate console tables, sets of shelves, or even a simple pinboard so that they look like small still-life arrangements.

Set the atmosphere with soft, low level lighting: adjustable dimmer switches can be easily fitted to bright overhead lights and bedside lamps to provide a gentle glow. Old fittings are often more interesting than their modern counterparts, but you must ensure that they are checked over by a qualified electrician. Cotton-covered electric cable looks more authentic than plastic cable and can be bought from specialty lighting stores. Candlelight is flattering and romantic: there are a host of period-style nightlights, lanterns, and wall sconces around, which come with the inevitable safety warning— "Never leave a lighted candle unattended"!

diamanté cushion

Textile designer Karen Nicol is an inveterate collector with the true expert's eye for the quirky and the unusual. Her studio is a real treasure trove, the accumulation of long hours spent scouring markets and yard sales for vintage costume jewelry, silk flowers, buttons, beads, and ribbons, all of which influence or are incorporated into her work. This sparkling cushion is a wonderful showcase for a collection of diamanté buckles, brooches, and dress clips.

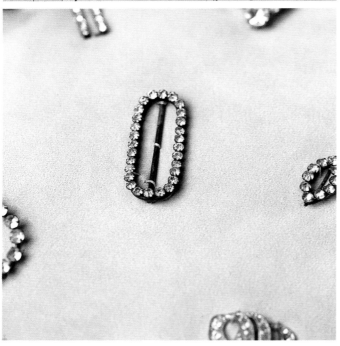

1 Clean all the pieces of jewelry with a soft cloth and check that all the paste jewels are securely fixed. Use a pair of small pliers to secure the settings as necessary.

MATERIALS AND EQUIPMENT

two 20-in. (50 cm) squares of fine soft suede or suede-look fabric

matching sewing thread

18-in. (45 cm) square cushion

19 brooches and buckles

low-tack masking tape

small pliers

sewing kit

2 Choose one of the larger items to be the center of the arrangement and place this in the middle of one suede square. Lay seven small buckles in a circle around it.

3 Arrange the remaining pieces around the edge in a circle, leaving a margin of at least 2 in. (5 cm) around the outside. The final look will depend very much upon the size and shape of your own jewelry.

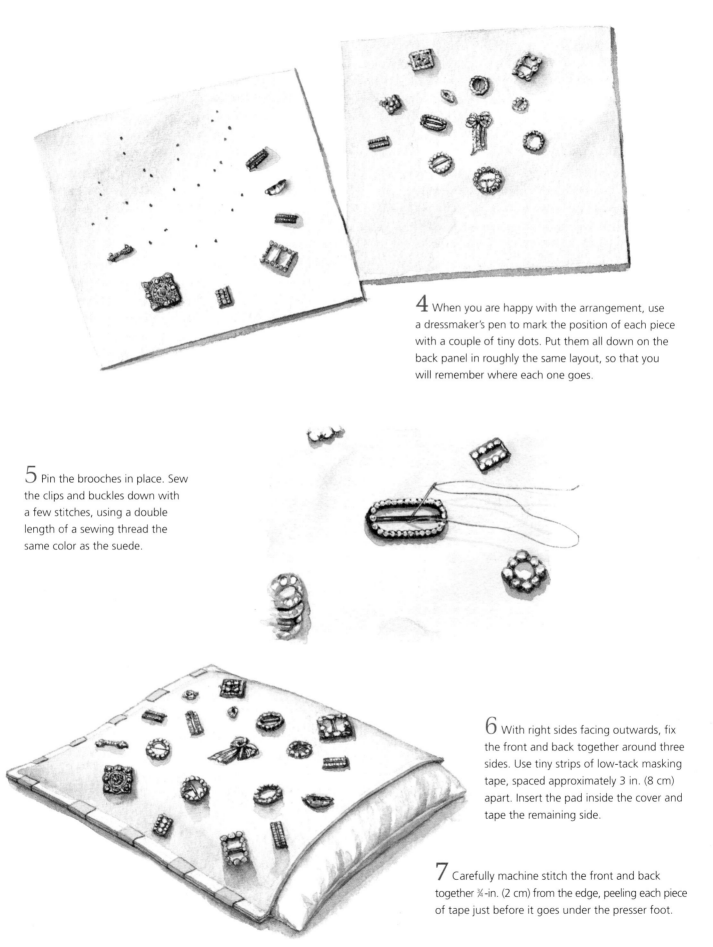

4 When you are happy with the arrangement, use a dressmaker's pen to mark the position of each piece with a couple of tiny dots. Put them all down on the back panel in roughly the same layout, so that you will remember where each one goes.

5 Pin the brooches in place. Sew the clips and buckles down with a few stitches, using a double length of a sewing thread the same color as the suede.

6 With right sides facing outwards, fix the front and back together around three sides. Use tiny strips of low-tack masking tape, spaced approximately 3 in. (8 cm) apart. Insert the pad inside the cover and tape the remaining side.

7 Carefully machine stitch the front and back together ¾-in. (2 cm) from the edge, peeling each piece of tape just before it goes under the presser foot.

bathrooms

Decades of modernization and makeovers mean that older homes rarely retain their original bathroom fixtures, but a few well-chosen period-style accessories will give a more relaxed ambience to the most spartan surroundings, and transform a clinical bathroom into a personal sanctuary for pampering and indulgence. Victorian houses and apartments often have bright, high-ceilinged bathrooms with sash windows and space for freestanding furniture, and these bathrooms were typically converted from a spare bedroom or dressing room. More modern, purpose-built bathrooms tend to be smaller and boxier, with fully fitted tub, sink, and toilet. Whatever the size, a classic white bathroom suite is the best starting point and, as with any other room, it is the choice of details that will create the overall atmosphere—whether you prefer an invigorating morning shower or a scented, candle-lit soak in essential oils at the end of the day.

ABOVE, LEFT Optimize your storage by using all the "hidden space" you can find, in an imaginative way. An old glass vitrine cabinet—of the type more usually found in a living room—has been painted with blue gloss and fixed into the shallow recess behind the head of the fitted paneled tub in this individual bathroom.

ABOVE, RIGHT A striking feature piece like this antique French enamel sink and splashback will always take center stage: maintain the impact by keeping to a plain color for the walls and flooring.

BELOW More atypical bathroom furniture: the combination of old wood and a claw-footed tub is cool and sophisticated.

key elements

Just as the bed is the dominant feature in any bedroom, the bathtub always sets the style for the bathroom. If your own tub is less than perfect, play it down by emphasising other aspects within the scheme, but if you are starting from scratch you will have a wide range from which to choose. Home improvement manuals from the mid-twentieth century exhorted householders to board in or replace resplendent Victorian tubs, but these are now highly desirable. The originals can be found in reclamation yards but may prove just too big and heavy for contemporary rooms (and impossible to get up the stairs). There are, fortunately, plenty of reproduction suites, some made on a smaller scale and all manufactured from lighter materials.

Freestanding furniture adds style to a larger bathroom, but if you do not have the space for a washstand, laundry hamper or set of drawers, you can create additional storage by installing a cupboard around the sink, or hanging towels from a wall- or ceiling-mounted rack. To end on a practical note, remember that all bathroom surfaces should be water-resistant to guard against splashes, dampness, and condensation. Varnish wooden furniture, seal floorboards, and use special "kitchen and bathroom" paints, which contain anti-fungicide for the walls.

THIS PICTURE Two model yachts perched on an airing rack and a few blue stripes are all it needs to create a nautical look.
INSET A life preserver, blue walls, and a tiny flotilla, overseen by Pinocchio, give an upbeat, more obviously seaside air to a family bathroom.

RIGHT Drawstring bags come in a range of sizes to contain anything from cosmetics to laundry. Save space by hanging them from handles or a peg rail.

MAIN PICTURE A full-length flowered curtain, made from easily washed unlined cotton, is the only element of pattern in this understated bathroom.

fabrics

Towels, shower curtains, and bathmats all have a functional role to play in the bathroom, but they do not have to be strictly utilitarian. Textiles are a good way to introduce color and pattern to a neutrally decorated bathroom, and they will also soften the effect of tiles, glass, and chrome. Vintage fabrics, in particular, can be used to emphasize existing period features, or to add character to a more modern bathroom.

Chintzy curtains always work well at windows, but they can also be used to cover the tub. Hem a panel to a same-sized waterproof shower curtain, insert eyelets along the top edge in corresponding positions, then fix the curtain rings through both curtains and hang in place.

Try mixing florals with the representational prints that were fashionable in the 1950s. These have a kitsch charm that is hard to resist: look out for ladylike patterns featuring lipsticks, perfume bottles, or powder compacts. Small remnants can be added to plain towels or made into simple drawstring bags. Old hand towels and individual guest towels made from waffle-weave fabric or huckaback are often embroidered with flowers or initials and finished off with crocheted lace. These look attractive when folded and hung from a clothes horse or wooden towel rail, even if they are not used daily.

ABOVE, LEFT A wide band of vintage 1950s furnishing fabric and a striped ribbon trim this plain hand towel.

ABOVE, RIGHT This pretty sheer curtain, perfect for screening a bathroom window, was made by stitching together a unique collection of vintage flower-printed handkerchiefs.

BELOW, RIGHT An eclectic assembly of textile prints adds color to the plain tiles of a 1930s bathroom.

BELOW, LEFT Edge a towel with a border of woven braid and white lace.

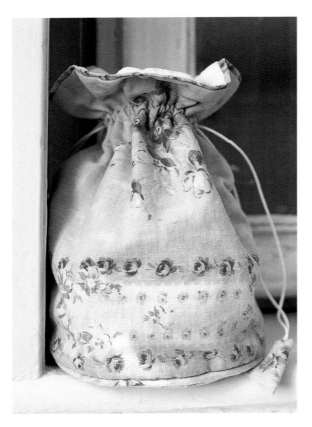

floral dorothy bag

Designer Caroline Zoob works from a studio in the English countryside, where she creates textile pieces with a fine attention to detail which all combine modern sensibility with a period style. She has an affinity with antique materials and made this drawstring bag—which is just right for holding your favorite cosmetics and toiletries—from a 1930s fabric remnant.

MATERIALS AND EQUIPMENT

antique fabric for the bag

white linen for the lining

16 in. (41 cm) length of piping cord

two 20 in. (50 cm) lengths of blind cord

matching sewing thread

sewing machine

sewing kit

small safety pin

CUTTING OUT

bag (antique fabric)

for the sides: two 8 x 9 in. (20 x 22 cm) rectangles

for the base: one 5½ in. (14 cm) diameter circle

1¼ x 16 in. (3 x 41 cm) border strip

1¼ x 16 in. (3 x 41 cm) bias strip cut with diagonal ends both sloping in the same direction for the piping

lining (white linen)

two 8 x 9 in. (20 x 22 cm) rectangles

one 5½ in. (14 cm) diameter circle

1 Mark the position of the drawstring channel with two points on each long side of each bag rectangle, 1¾ and 2¼ in. (4.5 and 5.5 cm) down from the top corners. With right sides facing, pin and tack together and join the long sides with a ½-in. (1 cm) seam, leaving the space between the marks unstitched. Press the seam open.

2 Join the short ends of the border strip, right sides facing, with a ½-in. (1 cm) seam. Press the seam open. With wrong sides facing, fold and press the border in half along the long edge. Turn the bag right side out, then pin and tack the border around the top, matching the raw edges and the seam.

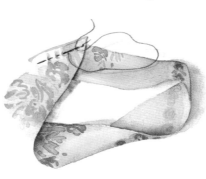

3 With right sides facing, sew the diagonal ends of the bias strip together to form a loop, then press the seam open.

4 Join the ends of the piping cord with slip stitch, overlapping them by ½ in. (1 cm). With wrong sides facing, fold the fabric loop in half over the cord and tack in place close to the cord.

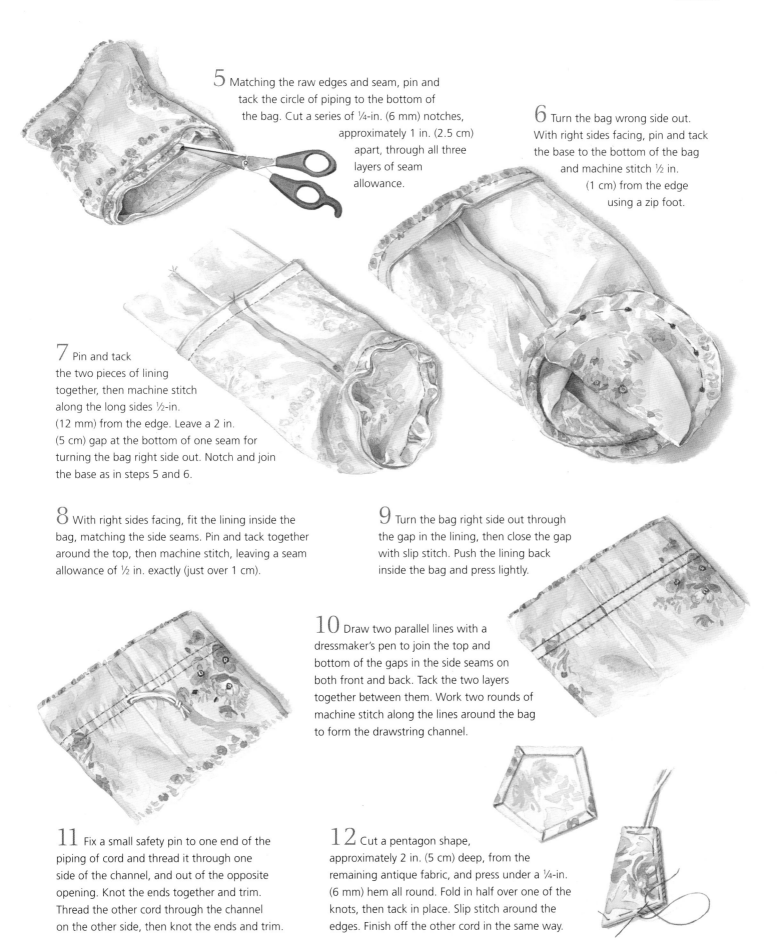

5 Matching the raw edges and seam, pin and tack the circle of piping to the bottom of the bag. Cut a series of ¼-in. (6 mm) notches, approximately 1 in. (2.5 cm) apart, through all three layers of seam allowance.

6 Turn the bag wrong side out. With right sides facing, pin and tack the base to the bottom of the bag and machine stitch ½ in. (1 cm) from the edge using a zip foot.

7 Pin and tack the two pieces of lining together, then machine stitch along the long sides ½-in. (12 mm) from the edge. Leave a 2 in. (5 cm) gap at the bottom of one seam for turning the bag right side out. Notch and join the base as in steps 5 and 6.

8 With right sides facing, fit the lining inside the bag, matching the side seams. Pin and tack together around the top, then machine stitch, leaving a seam allowance of ½ in. exactly (just over 1 cm).

9 Turn the bag right side out through the gap in the lining, then close the gap with slip stitch. Push the lining back inside the bag and press lightly.

10 Draw two parallel lines with a dressmaker's pen to join the top and bottom of the gaps in the side seams on both front and back. Tack the two layers together between them. Work two rounds of machine stitch along the lines around the bag to form the drawstring channel.

11 Fix a small safety pin to one end of the piping of cord and thread it through one side of the channel, and out of the opposite opening. Knot the ends together and trim. Thread the other cord through the channel on the other side, then knot the ends and trim.

12 Cut a pentagon shape, approximately 2 in. (5 cm) deep, from the remaining antique fabric, and press under a ¼-in. (6 mm) hem all round. Fold in half over one of the knots, then tack in place. Slip stitch around the edges. Finish off the other cord in the same way.

finishing touches

CENTER, LEFT Cluster small groups of attractive old and new perfume bottles on shelves or beside the sink.

CENTER, RIGHT This fine transfer-printed antique sink retains its original brass cross-head brass taps, which come complete with ceramic labels to distinguish "hot" from "cold": similar reproductions would give style to a modern sink.

BELOW, RIGHT When hanging items from a tiled wall, always fix the nail or screw into the grout so you can change the position or remove it.

BELOW, LEFT A hand towel with a woven, lettered border and a shell-shaped enamel soap dish will make a guest feel welcome and cared for.

TOP, LEFT Keep a spoon at hand to measure fragrant bath salts into steaming water.

TOP, RIGHT Shades of white on white always look chic and add a sense of space to the smallest bathroom.

OPPOSITE, ABOVE This striking patchwork splashback is made from a collection of blue and white Victorian tiles assembled over time.

OPPOSITE, BELOW RIGHT Antique cologne, smelling salt, and perfume bottles often have silver stoppers and collars: check the hallmark stamps to find out their exact age.

OPPOSITE, BELOW LEFT An array of luscious, rose-printed Edwardian postcards gives a facelift to a plain cream wall.

Bathroom accessories are not just limited to soap holders, towel rails, and medicine cabinets. All bathrooms have a mirror over the sink—it is essential for washing, shaving, and hairstyling—but additional mirrors can be positioned elsewhere to reflect sunshine back into a room, increasing the sense of space. Ornate picture frames make decorative alternatives to a plain mirror surround.

You can exhibit one-of-a-kind vintage finds such as old shaving brushes and soap dishes to great advantage against mirrors, shiny tiles, or along narrow shelves. Try decanting toiletries, essential oils, or bath salts into cut glass or colored bottles and jars, and arrange them along a windowsill where they will catch the sunlight, or show off exquisitely wrapped soaps in open baskets or small cupboards with wide open doors. Some packaging, especially that with retro-style labeling, is just too pretty to discard once empty: this too can be collected and displayed in your bathroom.

children's rooms

With great speed, a child's bedroom has to evolve from a simple nursery for sleeping into a private world of make-believe, then a den for playing with friends and, in time, a place for study and homework. With imagination, flexibility, and maybe a little nostalgia for your own childhood, you can meet these changing requirements, but take your child's own whims into account along the way. You may find yourself compromising with Thomas the Tank Engine curtains, or superhero comforter covers as young interior designers make their own contribution, but these tastes tend to pass quickly. The charms of pull-along wooden toys, wind-up trains, and irresistible teddy bears appeal to all ages, and shabby chic rose prints may, in the end, prove just as pleasing as Barbie-pink flounces.

MAIN PICTURE This lively room has a retro vibe but the combination of pastels, primaries, and off-white paintwork is undeniably contemporary.

INSET The pink chest of drawers—a revamped junkstore discovery— can easily be repainted in a few years if its young owner's tastes change.

key elements

Sleeping arrangements are the first consideration in any child's bedroom. Authentically vintage cots and beds do not meet modern safety requirements for babies and toddlers, but there are plenty of alternatives with which to create the look, including rush Moses baskets and oval cribs that convert into day beds. Save space with bunks for older siblings and pull-out trundle beds for sleepovers. Pretty antique single bedsteads—a favorite with young princesses—can be painted classic white, or with funkier vivid enamels.

A visit to any toystore will confirm the fact that children revel in bright colors. The shabbiest bureau can be revived with a coat of paint and, as long as you keep to similar tones, furniture painted in a mixture of colors will look vibrant and exciting. You can add additional layers of pattern with fabrics, but the inevitable accumulation of books, posters, and building bricks will bring a kaleidoscope of color in time. Fastidious parents, who prefer a more muted look, can try to keep this under control by planning ample storage. Old store units with many drawers, shallow boxes for under the bed, and high-level display shelving will all optimize space.

ABOVE, LEFT Every sleeping beauty needs her own fairytale chamber: this wooden hideaway has been built into the alcove beside a fireplace.

ABOVE, RIGHT Practical bunk beds maximize the floor area in this unfussy bedroom for two brothers.

RIGHT A giant bulletin board is an effective display solution. Copy the idea by stapling a remnant to a rectangle of soft board and securing it to the wall with picture plates. (Use magnetic boards as a spike-free alternative for small kids.)

71

LEFT Use three different printed fabrics in similar colors to upholster a characterful armchair. BELOW A stack of cushions and quilts softens an iron bedstead. BOTTOM, LEFT Crisp broderie anglaise pillows contrast with soft, faded rose-patterned quilts.

fabrics

Whether you are looking for strong primaries or faded pastels to set the scene in a child's room, you will find plenty of vintage inspiration in stores selling both old and new textile pieces. If you search in the right places, there are still many original cotton curtains, bedspreads, and dressing-table covers featuring prints of 1950s cowboys, racing cars, and seaside scenes to be unearthed. Many of these designs are now being reproduced, as manufacturers follow the lead of Cath Kidston, the doyenne of vintage domesticity.

You may also find antique bedlinen, which has already been used by four generations but which still has much wear remaining. The smaller scale of children's bedding means that damaged sheets can be cut down and re-hemmed and, for the truly thrifty, offcuts can be stitched into cushion covers, tiny padded hearts or used in patchwork. Many old down comforters and quilts have survived as family heirlooms, but there also lots of new versions around, many hand-stitched in India, which will better withstand daily wear and tear.

Checkered and striped fabrics, from any era and on every scale from pinstripe shirting to harlequin diamonds, are perennial favorites for children. They always look bright and cheerful, and can be mixed and matched with patterns or with florals to create a variety of themed looks from folk art to nautical.

MAIN PICTURE Ticking stripes and gingham checks in nautical red, white, and blue would be ideal for either a boy's or girl's room. This color scheme is one which will grow up with the child, as the soft toys are replaced with more sophisticated accessories.

FAR LEFT This woolen patchwork can be made very quickly. Edge each square with blanket stitch in contrasting tapestry yarn and join them together with slip stitch.
LEFT If you do not have a crocheter in the family, check out thrift stores for bright afghan throws.

MATERIALS AND EQUIPMENT

selection of printed handkerchiefs

white bias binding

ric-rac braid

narrow gingham ribbon

decorative buttons

matching sewing thread

sewing kit

handkerchief curtain

The treasured collection of printed hankies I used in making this hand-stitched curtain dates back to my childhood in the 1970s. Boxed sets of seven, one for each day of the week, were popular gifts from my grandparents and great-aunts, who were anxious to encourage polite behaviour. The charming illustrations range from nursery rhyme characters and Mabel Lucie Attwell pixies to Bugs Bunny and Tweety Pie. (The bathroom curtain on page 63 was put together in a similar way.)

1 Wash and press the handkerchiefs, then lay them out on the floor to match the size and shape of the window, allowing an extra 6 in. (15 cm) across the width to create a little fullness when the curtain is hung.

2 Line up whole handkerchiefs along the bottom edge, then trim others to size as necessary to give a straight top.

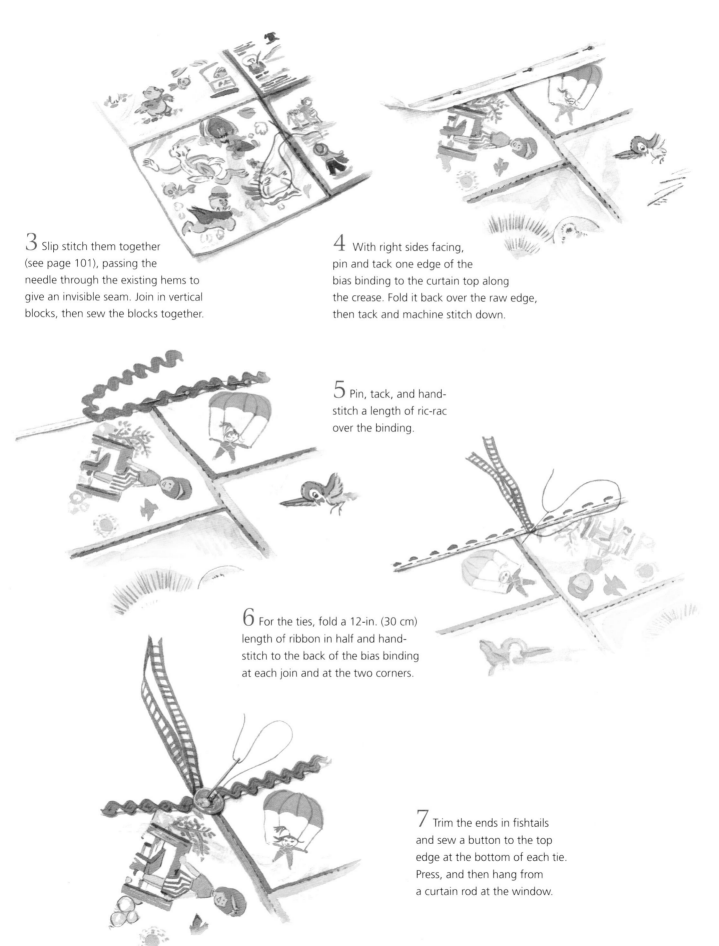

3 Slip stitch them together (see page 101), passing the needle through the existing hems to give an invisible seam. Join in vertical blocks, then sew the blocks together.

4 With right sides facing, pin and tack one edge of the bias binding to the curtain top along the crease. Fold it back over the raw edge, then tack and machine stitch down.

5 Pin, tack, and hand-stitch a length of ric-rac over the binding.

6 For the ties, fold a 12-in. (30 cm) length of ribbon in half and hand-stitch to the back of the bias binding at each join and at the two corners.

7 Trim the ends in fishtails and sew a button to the top edge at the bottom of each tie. Press, and then hang from a curtain rod at the window.

finishing touches

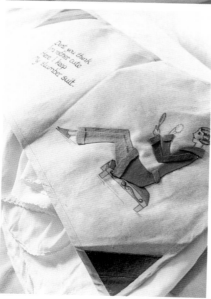

Children are instinctive collectors, and feel reassured when surrounded by their favorite possessions. Make the most of this squirrelling habit by providing plenty of places for display, along with chests or boxes in which to keep prized keepsakes. Toys are meant to be played with, and if you have childhood mementos stowed away—a tattered teddy bear, a baby buggy, toy fort, or rocking horse—this is the place to show them off and share them with your own children. Hand-knitted or -crocheted animals and dolls enjoy almost cult status now and are often to be found at yard sales and flea markets, along with other vintage toys.

Tiny garments can be put out on view and displayed against the wall or on the back of the door. If space is at a premium, install two or more wooden peg rails beside the cot and hang up dresses, petticoats, and homemade cardigans from small-sized hangers—this looks attractive and also means everything is at hand at getting up time. You can encourage imaginative play by keeping the family's unwanted clothes, hats, and bags in a special place ready for dressing-up games, along with spare blankets, throws and lengths of cloth. Never forget that an ordinary pile of cushions may be used to construct a giant's castle and a rag rug can always turn into a flying carpet.

OPPOSITE ABOVE, FAR LEFT Make the most of your walls by hanging up artwork with clothespins screwed to a wooden rail and hanging dresses from peg rails.

OPPOSITE ABOVE, LEFT Tiny fingers enjoy playing with miniature collections—display them within the compartments of a paper-covered printer's tray.

OPPOSITE CENTER, FAR LEFT Hang a row of sunhats from pegs.

OPPOSITE CENTER, LEFT A floppy-eared rabbit, made from a scrap of dress material, will be a lifelong friend.

OPPOSITE BELOW, FAR LEFT Scraps of bright stitchery cut from worn mats or napkins can be reused to make patchwork pieces.

OPPOSITE BELOW, LEFT This glamorous 1920s lady appears on the pages of a grown-up rag book.

THIS PAGE A unifying color will always pull the look together. Here a pretty bedroom chair and a battered doll's buggy share the same pale shell pink. The gilt-framed antique mirror is an elegant feature, much appreciated by a little girl with stylish tastes.

pull-along duck

This little white painted duck, which is made from a piece of reclaimed floorboard, has a traditional charm that will appeal to all small children—and their parents. Once it is no longer played with, it is bound to become a special memento, to be treasured and passed on to the next generation.

MATERIALS AND EQUIPMENT

enough ½-in. (1 cm) wood to cut the following pieces:

two 5 x 7½-in. (13 cm x 19 cm), for body and head

one 7 x 3½-in. (17 x 9 cm), for base

two 2½ x 4-in. (6 x 10 cm), for wings

enough ⅓-in. (8 mm) wood to make four 2-in. (5 cm) diameter circles, for wheels

2 wooden buttons with back loops, for eyes

1 large wooden bead for cord

wooden dowelling, for wing and wheel dowels

4-in. (10 cm) of ¼-in. (6 mm) 12-in. (30 cm) thick twine

tracing paper · pencil

G-clamps · jigsaw

drill with ¼-in. (6 mm) and ¹⁄₁₂-in. (2 mm) twist bits

medium and fine sandpaper

sanding block (optional)

scrap wood · ruler · screwdriver

wood glue · hammer

10-in. (25 cm) shirring elastic

2-in. (5 cm) No. 10 wood screw

NOTE This toy should not be given to a child under 36 months.

1 Trace the templates on page 103 and transfer all except the wheels on to the floorboard, remembering to include all the X-marks. Draw the wheels on the thin wood.

4 Make four X-marks on the edges of the long sides of the base, 1¼-in. (3 cm) in from the ends. Holding the base secure with G-clamps, drill four ¼-in. (6 mm) axle holes through the X- marks, 1¼ in. (3 cm) into the base.

2 With G-clamps, attach the wood firmly to a workbench. Use a jigsaw to cut out all the shapes. Then, using a drill fitted with a ¼-in. (6 mm) bit, make a hole through each wheel for the axle dowels.

3 Sand each shape with medium then fine sandpaper, rounding off all the corners and edges to achieve a smooth finish ready for painting. When sanding the flat surfaces, you may find it helpful to wrap the sandpaper around a sanding block.

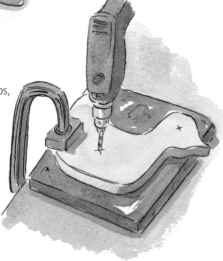

5 Place a piece of scrap wood underneath the duck's body to protect your work surface and secure both pieces to the bench with G-clamps. Using a ¹⁄₁₂-in. (2 mm) bit, drill holes at the X-mark through the head for the eyes, and through the center of the body for the wings. Drill similar holes halfway through the thickness of the wings, on the inside. The pieces should now be painted before assembly (see page 103).

6 Paint all the shapes with one coat of white acrylic primer, then let dry for an hour. When dry, rub back with sandpaper to allow some of the grain to show through. Paint the base and the buttons for the eyes blue. Paint the wheels, beak and bead with cadmium orange. When dry, sand back each of the painted pieces to reveal some of the grain.

7 Cut a length of $1/12$-in. (2 mm) dowelling to fit through the body and halfway into each wing. Put a drop of glue into the drilled hole in the body, then carefully tap the dowel through with a hammer. Tap the wings on to the dowels so they fit snugly.

8 To make the eyes, knot the shirring elastic to the shank of one button, then thread the other end through the hole in the duck's head. Stretch the elastic and, maintaining the tension, tie it firmly to the other button. Trim the ends, apply glue to both button backs, and release the elastic to hold the buttons securely in place.

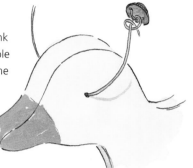

9 To make the axles, cut the $1/4$ in. (6 mm) dowelling into four $2\frac{1}{2}$ in. (6 cm) lengths, so that they fit into the holes in the base and through both wheels, leaving $3/4$-in. (2 cm) of dowel extending beyond each wheel. Paint blue and, when dry, drill a $1/12$-in. (2 mm) hole about $1/3$-in. (8 mm) from one end of each piece to take the wheel dowels. Put a little glue on the other end of each dowel, then tap them through the axle holes with a hammer. Slide a wheel on each. To make the wheel dowels, cut the remaining thin doweling into four $1/2$-in. (1 cm) lengths and paint blue. When dry, glue one in each axle dowels to hold the wheels.

10 To secure the duck to the base, drill a hole up through the base, as marked. Then drill a smaller hole in the bottom of the duck to take the screw. Attach the base to the duck, using the large wood screw.

11 Drill a hole through the front of the base, as marked, to take the twine. Tie a knot in one end of the twine, thread the cord through the hole, then through the large bead. Tie a second knot at the other end of the twine to secure the bead. Apply a thin layer of glue to both knots to prevent them unraveling.

workrooms

Mundane tasks—arranging deliveries, paying bills, patching worn jeans—are an inevitable part of the daily routine and most households at least have a corner set aside for the sewing basket, phone directories, and a row of filing boxes, if not a dedicated study. Modern communications, however, mean that additional space now has to be found for all the essential technology that goes with working from home, ordering online, and doing homework. A vintage-style workroom should look like an integral part of your home, not an impersonal office full of bulky equipment and dull files, so stow your laptop away in a drawer and keep printers, scanners, faxes, and sewing machines out of sight in cupboards or concealed behind a screen. You can then turn your attention to collecting and displaying the accessories and furniture that will create a lived-in, more congenial atmosphere for your working area.

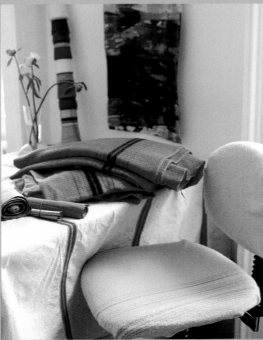

key elements

Think laterally when planning a home workroom and utilize what you have at hand: any table can be used as a work surface, and woven shopping baskets or leather suitcases will house paperwork and stationery. If you prefer a more functional look, however, reclaimed and restored office furniture is easy to come by and adapts well to a domestic setting. Classic items like architect's plan chests and huge leather-topped partner's desks look great if you have the space, but smaller-scale writing tables and oak kneehole desks are equally attractive. Mid-twentieth-century metal desks, filing cabinets, and lockers, reminiscent of civil service office suppliers, take on a cool, contemporary look when stripped of paint and polished to a dull sheen.

Well thought out lighting and supportive seating are important design elements if you are going to spend a long time writing, using a computer, or sewing. There are plenty of old, new, and reproduction desk lamps to choose from: the iconic anglepoise, first designed over 70 years ago, is still the most stylish of these. An authentic swivel chair is the perfect partner for a vintage desk, and sleeker than its modern counterpart... but you may need to place a cushion on the seat to add a little home comfort.

ABOVE, LEFT This well-planned homework area for an older child sits discreetly in a corner without dominating the bedroom. Now a design classic, the 1970s wall-mounted storage unit is the perfect way to keep stationery, keys, pencils, and pens at hand without cluttering the desktop. The smooth curved shapes accentuate the functional lines of the desk and vintage yellow chair, while a bright-red desk light and an old record box add more primary color to the neutral background.

BELOW, LEFT The filing cabinet, metal anglepoise desk lamp, and old mesh wastepaper basket in this relaxed work space could have come straight from an office, but the battered wooden kitchen table, fresh flowers, and quirky touches, such as the luggage labels tied onto the drawer handles, reveal the more homey setting. The table has been positioned within a bay window to make the most of the bright daylight and to provide a constantly changing view of the outside world.

LEFT A clever use of space in a loft conversion: the wide shelf directly under the dormer window acts as a desk, while the lower one provides plenty of extra storage.

MAIN PICTURE A splendid, vast filing cabinet, over-head lighting, and a row of old office chairs, set on either side of a refectory table, give a purposeful air to this design studio.

LEFT This wonderful old adjustable tailor's dummy is still put to its original use in a light-filled sewing room, but would look equally effective as an unusual display stand for favorite items of clothing, jewelry and hats.

BELOW, LEFT These ornamental hatboxes double up as storage containers for remnants of fabric. Arranged within an empty fireplace alcove, alongside a hand sewing machine and a basket of scraps, they provide an eye-catching focal point in a busy workroom.

fabrics

You do not have to be a textile artist or a dressmaker to enjoy collecting vintage fabrics and sewing notions: most people who enjoy needlework have their own personal hoard of materials, buttons, lace and ribbons, old silk scarves, and embroidered napkins. Instead of storing these away in boxes, they can be put out on display in a sewing room or work area as a source of inspiration for future projects or just to be enjoyed for their unique qualities.

Glass-fronted draper's drawers are the perfect place to keep remnants and larger pieces of cloth, but these can also be folded and grouped together by color, pattern, or size, then stacked in wicker baskets or on open shelves. Clear jars, especially the larger ones, which once held candies, make ideal containers for small scraps, buttons and beads. Professional designers will always have a "mood board" as a source of inspiration in their studio, on which they pin favorite postcards, swatches, samples, and lengths of braid and ribbons—a decorative idea that can be copied at home. Fabrics can also be used make a study or workroom less office-like. Make sure you have attractive curtains, covers, and cushions surrounding you, and use flower-printed or striped offcuts or sample lengths to disguise dull files and notebooks.

TOP, LEFT A pretty flowered chintz slipcover will protect a well-loved but dog-eared novel from further wear and tear.

TOP, CENTER Roll-up "housewives" like this have been used for many years to store sewing scissors, buttons, and needles. Make your own from a strip of flannel or fabric lined with silk and fitted with small pockets and tape loops in which to slot small items.

TOP, RIGHT This brocade drawstring pouch contains antique needlework tools: the Dorothy bag (on page 64) would also make a useful sewing-kit holder.

ABOVE, LEFT AND RIGHT Colorful pearl-headed pins are easier to use and prettier than plain steel dressmaker's pins.

LEFT Humble shoeboxes or purpose-made box files can be covered with remnants of floral fabric and displayed on shelves.

finishing touches

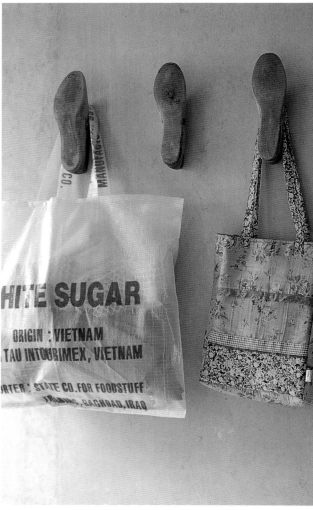

ABOVE, LEFT Fine hand writing has period charm: glue photocopied letters onto plain boxes and files.

ABOVE, CENTER Turn plain writing paper into something special with simple details like these rows of pressed flowers.

ABOVE, RIGHT A length of silky ribbon and a drop pearl fastening add a touch of glamour.

BELOW, RIGHT Three antique wooden shoe lasts, screwed securely into the wall, make idiosyncratic hangers.

BELOW, LEFT A gold ribbon can be tied around a bundle of love letters.

LEFT, CENTER The fastenings on these boxes are made from fine twine looped over linen buttons. The stamped numbers could easily be copied onto a pile of new boxes.

FAR RIGHT White-painted typesetters' drawers, with their many compartments, make good display cases.

Once you have settled on the furniture and soft furnishings for your sewing room or study, it is time to plan the final details. You will doubtless need some ordinary stationery supplies—ring binders, a calculator, a stapler, and a hole puncher—which are essential but far from stimulating to look at, so these can be simply bundled away into interesting tote bags or plastic bags saved from your travels (as shown on the left) and hung up on the wall.

To complete the look, there are a few accessories that always evoke a traditional office environment. A round-faced schoolroom clock with large numerals, a wire mesh wastepaper basket, a metal fan to keep you cool, or a stack of wooden in-trays all have an authentic, hard-working appeal. A letter rack, like that on pages 88–89, is always useful and can be painted to match your room scheme or covered in photocopied manuscript to match the magazine file, opposite. Paintbrushes and pencils can be kept at hand on the desk in mugs or stoneware jars and, if you really want to return to a less frenetic age, you could buy a reconditioned vintage telephone, a blotting pad, a fountain pen, and a bottle of ink.

letter rack

A useful aid to keeping track of your correspondence, Sally and Stewart Walton's rack has separate compartments for both incoming and outgoing letters. It is made out of fiberboard, with a wooden bead trim around the base.

1 Enlarge the templates on page 103 and transfer the shapes onto the MDF board. Clamp the wood to a workbench using G-clamps. Wearing a face mask, cut each shape out carefully with a jigsaw, and then sand any rough edges.

MATERIALS AND EQUIPMENT

enough ¼ in. (6 mm) MDF to cut the following pieces:

one 2⅞ x 9⅛ in. (7.3 x 23 cm), for front

one 6⅛ x 9⅛ in. (15.5 x 23 cm), for back

one 4⅜ x 8⅝ in. (11 x 21.8 cm), for central divider

two 6⅛ x 2¾ in. (15.5 x 7 cm), for sides

one approximately 9⅛ x 3¼ in. (23 x 8.2 cm) for base (cut to fit)

24 in. (60 cm) length of ⅝ in. (1.5 cm) triangular beading, to surround front and sides of base

tracing paper • pencil

G-clamps • workbench

face mask • jigsaw

medium and fine sandpaper

wood glue • panel pins • hammer

tenon saw • miter box

2 To assemble the rack, apply wood glue to the edges of the side pieces and butt them up to the back and front pieces. Clamp these joints until the glue has bonded, then reinforce with panel pins tapped through from the front and back into the sides.

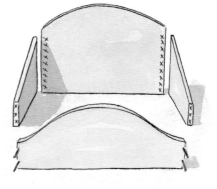

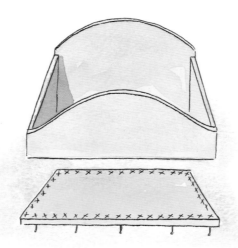

3 Place the assembled rack on the MDF and draw around the bottom edge. Cut out the base around this line (wearing the mask), apply wood glue to the bottom edge of the rack and clamp it in position. Pin through from underneath to reinforce.

4 Mark the position of the central divider on the side pieces. Apply wood glue to the side and bottom edges and slip it in place (see opposite).

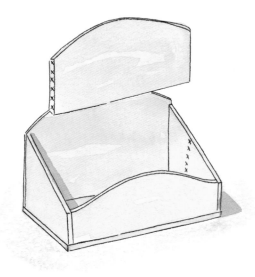

5 Using a tenon saw, cut three lengths of beading to fit snugly around the front and sides of the base, mitering the corners at 45 degrees with a miter box.

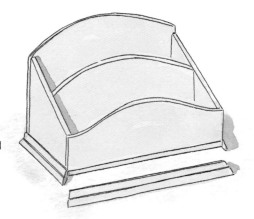

6 Glue the beading in position, placing the rack on a flat surface so that the base is level. Clamp in position until the glue has bonded.

PAINT PALETTE AND EQUIPMENT

white acrylic primer

artists' acrylic paints in the following colors:

chocolate brown

Venetian red · ultramarine

black · white · gray

water-based satin varnish

shallow white container, for mixing

broad long-handled paintbrush

cardboard box, for spray-booth

stiff-bristled paintbrush

varnishing brush

Paint swatches

Chocolate brown

Venetian red

Blue-black (optional)
   3 parts ultramarine
   1 part black

Pink
   3 parts Venetian red
   1 part white

Gray
   3 parts gray
   1 part ultramarine

Steps to paint

1 Paint the whole rack with white acrylic primer, using a broad long-handled paintbrush to get down into the divisions. Let dry.

2 Again using a long-handled brush, apply the chocolate brown base coat and let it dry.

3 Make a simple three-sided spray-booth out of a large cardboard box.

4 Practice your spattering technique on scrap paper: load the stiff-bristled paintbrush with paint, then run your finger across the top to flick dots of paint on to the surface. Some dots will be bigger than others, but try not to make them too big or the paint will run and spoil the effect. Flick first with Venetian red, then with a blue-black, if you decide to use it, then with pink, and finally with gray. Let dry.

5 When you are satisfied with the overall effect, apply two coats of water-based satin varnish according to the manufacturer's instructions.

outdoors

Despite the vagaries of the climate, outdoor life is increasingly popular and the boundaries between house and garden often become blurred during the summer months. The garden is no longer just a place to hang out the washing or grow vegetables: spaces from orchards and overgrown lawns to urban backyards have been transformed into relaxed living areas where we can laze, dine, play, and just enjoy looking at the trees, plants and wildlife.

Always informal and individual, contemporary vintage style works particularly well outdoors. Faded chintz, long-used garden furniture, squashy cushions, and patchwork quilts look at home amid lush green foliage and scented flowers. Authentic garden antiques are comparatively rare and not always in the best condition, so look out for affordable reproductions or give a distressed finish to new pieces— this is the perfect place to mix old and new.

key elements

Garden furniture is essential for *alfresco* eating and socializing, and there are many old and vintage-style tables and chairs, in both wood and metal, from which to choose. Genuine antiques, with attractively weathered or distressed surfaces, have survived many years of use and blend well with the natural textures of wooden fencing, stone terraces, or brick walls. If you are buying new furniture, painted wood will inevitably peel if left out for long enough, while benches made from reddish-brown hardwoods fade to a silvery gray in time.

Architectural salvage yards are a good hunting ground for furniture and also other horticultural items such as cold frames, wrought iron gates, metal rollers, and cloches, which may be put to their original purpose, or treated as objets d'art. If you want to create hard landscaping within the garden, try cladding walls or patios with reclaimed paving slabs, granite sets, and slate tiles. Authentic garden statuary and hand-thrown terracotta pots are sought after and expensive. Cast concrete or terracotta reproductions will become encrusted with lichens and moss in time, but you can always imitate the aging process with a coat of diluted white or colored latex paint.

ABOVE, LEFT A row of large color-washed terracotta plant pots, spilling over with pelargoniums, has been arranged on a low wall, where it casts shade across a secluded work space and makes an informal divider between indoors and outdoors.

ABOVE, RIGHT Old tools are too interesting to be consigned to the back of the potting shed. Galvanized watering cans and containers, a sieve, trowels, forks, and even a birdhouse appeal to the armchair gardener as well as the green-fingered.

LEFT The original faded blue paintwork on these louver shutters, the scuffed planks and the old wooden chair set off the adjacent urn.

MAIN PICTURE Remove old paintwork from vintage furniture with chemical stripper, a scraper, and a wire brush, then rub down with steel wool before repainting.

RIGHT The mesh seats of these sinuous chairs were designed so water drains easily. They can be left outdoors all year round, but metal furniture needs special attention.

THIS PICTURE Improvise a sun canopy for a day bed by stringing spare sheets or lengths of billowing sheer fabric between a tree and a bamboo pole.

ABOVE, LEFT The muted tones of this rose-printed cushion, quilt, and knitted throw seem to merge into their green environment.

ABOVE, CENTER To measure up for these pads add 4 in. (10 cm) to the dimensions of the seat, then make a cushion as on page 101.

ABOVE, RIGHT For this engaging clothespin bag, cut and bind an opening across a child's jersey, seam the bottom, and insert a small hanger.

BELOW Lounging in a hammock is the epitome of summer ease—make yourself even snugger with plenty of cushions and a quilt.

fabrics

Look to your surroundings and take nature as your inspiration when selecting textiles for outside spaces. Strong colors and bold shapes look at home by the sea or in a sun-drenched backyard, while sprigged florals echo the varied planting and dappled green shade of a country plot. All soft furnishings take on a more informal appearance when they are put outside, so use them to add comfort and individuality to your garden.

Dress up old metal chairs with flowery seat pads and drape a matching cloth over a garden table to set the scene for lunch. Folding wooden seating—deckchairs or director's chairs—can be given an aged look by replacing the existing slings with vintage-style fabric, cut and seamed to the same size. Repaint the framework to match. Lay a quilt over a plastic dust sheet pile it with cushions, and then picnic—or just stretch out on the lawn. Parasols, awnings, and canopies all provide welcome shade and are usually made from weather-resistant acrylic cloth, specially designed for outdoor use. Soften the look by re-covering or draping them with patterned remnants, but remember that the sun will fade (and dampness will rot) any fabrics left out for too long.

finishing touches

TOP, LEFT Polkadot ceramic tumblers make a colorful alternative to ordinary flowerpots for these bright-yellow marigolds.

TOP, RIGHT A mid-twentieth-century design classic, this white-painted wire chair by Harry Bertoia brings 1950s style to a suburban garden.

CENTER, LEFT Plant stands and baskets fashioned from ornately woven wirework were immensely popular in Victorian gardens and conservatories; see how to make your own simplified version in the project overleaf.

CENTER, RIGHT This somewhat startled pottery hen has been given a new purpose as a plant holder.

BELOW, LEFT Another imaginative reuse of an old container: a stenciled hot-water jug holds a pretty verbena.

BELOW, RIGHT Any design motif becomes more effective when repeated. Here, a row of four "brown betty" teapots makes a strong impact on a weathered windowsill.

OPPOSITE, ABOVE RIGHT Keep an eye out for old wooden storage crates with stenciled lettering.

OPPOSITE, BELOW LEFT Although your garden may be full of flowering plants, a handful of cut stems will always add extra interest to the table.

OPPOSITE, BELOW RIGHT A functional old galvanized bucket serves as a useful garden trug.

As outdoor living is redefined, gardens and patios have become open-air extensions, to be decorated with the same care and attention as an interior. Whatever its size, there will always be room for the quirky items that give character and individuality. In addition to displaying old equipment, such as cloches, propagating trays, and splendidly dented watering cans or imported olive jars and amphorae, this is the place to recycle domestic items that are no longer suitable for daily use. Think laterally: anything from a lidless coffee pot or a cracked jug to a plastic shopping tote bag can double up as a container: simply add drainage and compost, then fill with plants. At night time you can set the scene for a romantic dinner by hanging up strings of outdoor Christmas lights, insect-repellent citronella candles, shadow lanterns, or simple tea lights in empty glass jam jars—and keep yourself warm with a fashionable chimenea fireplace or café-style gas heaters.

wirework basket

This wirework basket by Jane Seabrook is more of an enclosure than a container; such edgings were used in the early nineteenth century as a feature surround for garden plants. A strip of galvanized iron, bent into a circle, creates the framework for the miniature fence that supports the bushes. The best roses to use are low-growing ground cover varieties, but you can adapt the size of the planter to accommodate larger shrub roses. Be sure to wear protective gloves when making this project.

MATERIALS AND EQUIPMENT

1 sheet of galvanized iron, 48 x 12 in. (120 x 30 cm) use a gauge than can be cut with tin snips

6 galvanized roofing bolts, ½ in. (1 cm) long and ¼ in. (6 mm) wide

25 yd. (23 m) of ⅛ in. (5 mm) thick galvanized fencing wires

20 x 14 in. (50 x 35 cm) rectangle of 1 in. (2.5 cm) plywood tin snips

hacksaw and vice or G-clamps

jigsaw

gray-blue metal primer

well-rotted manure and rose fertilizer

5 bare-root rose plants (*Rosa* "The Fairy")

Making the basket

1 Cut the sheet of iron into 4-in. (10 cm) wide strips, two at 48 in. (120 cm) long and one at 24 in. (60 cm) long.

2 Drill two ⅜-in. (7 mm) diameter holes in the same positions at the ends of each strip. Fix the three sections together to form a ring by lining up the holes and securing the joins with roofing bolts. This strip acts as a template for preparing the bed and as a retainer for the basket.

3 For the basket, cut the fencing wire into sixteen 55-in. (140 cm) lengths with a hacksaw. Use a vice or G-clamp to hold the wire in place when cutting.

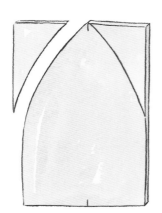

4 To shape the wire, you will need to make a former from the plywood; this will act as a solid template around which to bend one into shape. Mark the top center point and draw the curved sides to within 8 in. (20 cm) of the base. Cut out the shape with a jigsaw.

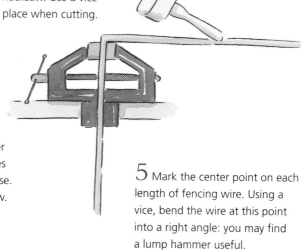

5 Mark the center point on each length of fencing wire. Using a vice, bend the wire at this point into a right angle: you may find a lump hammer useful.

6 Place this right angle over the point of the former and bend the wire to fit the template exactly. The wire should extend for about 4 in. (10 cm) beyond the lower edge of the former.

7 Each section of the planter now needs to be bent outwards in a curve. Turn the arches sideways and use the former to guide the curve into shape.

8 Before constructing the basket, paint all the metal components with metal primer. The gray blue used here appears as a patinated copper color and provides a good foil for the pink roses.

Preparing and planting the bed

9 Choose an area of flat ground for your rose bed. If the area is grassed over, position the ring and cut around its inner edge to mark the turf. Put the ring aside and remove the turf by dividing it into squares and lifting out with a spade. Turn over the bed and fork in the manure, and then gently press the ring into position.

10 Plant the five roses, positioning them according to the planting plan (right). Make sure the junction of stem and root are at surface level. Top dress with rose fertilizer.

Assembling the basket

11 Insert the first wire arch hard up against the inner edge of the ring with the tip bending outwards and push it about 6–8 in. (15–20 cm) into the ground. Position the next arch so that it overlaps the first one by half its width. Repeat this process for the remaining arches all the way around the circumference of the ring; you may need to adjust the spacing on some of the wires for a neat and even fit.

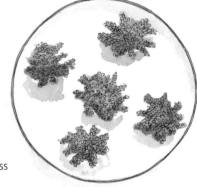

12 Secure the basket sections together by twisting lengths of thin galvanized wire around the crossover junctions on each arch.

13 Prune the roses so that they form a slightly domed shape, and trim back any grass around the outer edge for a formal effect.

Alternative planting schemes

Try the roses "White Pet" or "Nozomi" for a container of this size or, for a larger arrangement, use the pink rose "Marguerite Hilling" or its creamy-white sister "Nevada." A suitable flowering shrub would be *Camellia japonica* "Alba Plena."

techniques

SEWING KIT

The equipment and sewing notions needed for most needlework is minimal, but it is worth investing in the best tools to help you achieve lasting and professional results.

Modern sewing machines have many advanced features, but the projects in this book require only a basic straight stitch and a zigzag for neatening seams. It is useful to have several pairs of scissors, each with its own purpose, such as dressmaking shears, paper scissors, and embroidery scissors. Your sewing box should also contain a selection of needles, a thimble, dressmaker's pins and a fading or water-soluble dressmaker's pen for transferring marks.

SEAMS AND HEMS

If you can hem the edges of a length of fabric and join two pieces together, you have mastered the basic techniques of sewing and should be able to tackle all of the step-by-step projects described in the earlier chapters.

1 Plain seam

The extra fabric needed to join two edges is given as the seam allowance. To keep the seam consistent, match the raw edges to the corresponding line on the machine's baseplate when stitching. With right sides facing, line up the two edges and pin at 2–4 in. (5–10 cm) intervals. Tack, then machine stitch along the seam line. Unpick the tacking, then press the seam open or over to one side, as directed.

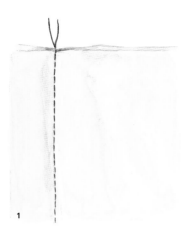

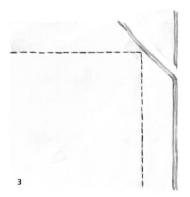

2 Neatened seam

Raw fabric edges may fray, especially if an item is washed, but this can be prevented by neatening the seam. If it is to be pressed open, zigzag or overlock each cut edge before seaming. If the seam is to be pressed to one side, the allowance can be trimmed and the two edges zigzagged together (as shown left).

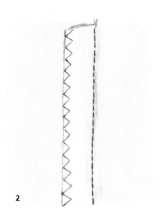

3 Sewing around a corner

Stitch to the end of the seam allowance and, keeping the needle down, raise the presser foot. Turn the fabric through 90 degrees and continue sewing. Clip off the corner to within ⅛-in. (3 mm) of the stitching before turning through so that it will lie flat.

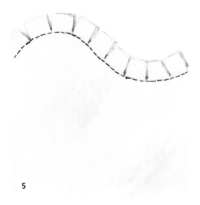

4 Double hem

This consists of one narrow and one deeper turning or two equal-sized turnings (which give a firmer edge to finer fabrics). Press the two folds under and pin, then tack in place. Machine stitch close to the inner fold or finish by hand with slip stitch (see 7, opposite) if you do not want the stitching to show on the right side.

5 Curved seam

The allowance on a curved join has to be trimmed back to ½-in. (1 cm) and clipped so that the seam will lie flat. On an outside curve make small notches. On an inside curve, snip a short distance into the allowance at regular intervals.

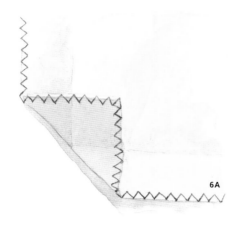

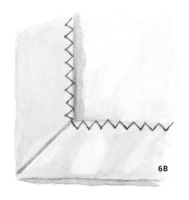

6 Mitered corner

When two hems meet at right angles, the surplus fabric is neatened with a miter to avoid bulk. Press the turnings under, then unfold. Fold each corner inwards and press so the creases line up to make a square (as shown). Refold the hems, then slip stitch the folded edges together (see left). For a double hem, unfold the second turning only before refolding and stitching.

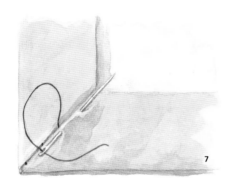

7 Slip stitch

Slip stitch is used for joining two folded edges where they meet, for example, at a mitered corner or along the opening of a simple cushion cover, and also to secure a double hem. Bring the needle out through the fold and pick up two threads of the other fabric on the other side with the point. Pass the needle back through the first fold for ¼ in. (6 mm) and repeat to the end.

CUSHIONS AND PILLOWS

Ready-made pads to go inside cushions or pillows, with feather or synthetic fillings, come in a range of shapes and many sizes.

1 Basic cushion cover

The simplest covers are closed with slip stitch. This has to be unpicked and resewn for cleaning, but it is almost invisible, especially if the seams are piped. Covers should be the same dimensions as the pad, without any extra seam allowance, to give the cushion a well-stuffed look. Cut two pieces of fabric the same size as the pad. Add piping if required, then pin and tack the edges together with right sides facing. Machine stitch, leaving a 10 in. (25 cm) gap along one side. Clip the corners, turn right side out and press. Press under the unstitched seam allowance. Insert the pad and slip stitch the opening with matching thread.

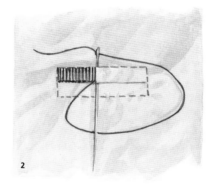

2 Buttoned fastenings

If you want to add a row of buttons to an envelope back, the opening will need to be reinforced, so allow a 2 in. (5 cm) double hem along each edge (see opposite). Mark the button positions along the center of one hem and make matching vertical buttonholes on the other panel by hand or by machine. Make up the cover as described in 1, pinning on the buttonhole panel first, then sew on the buttons.

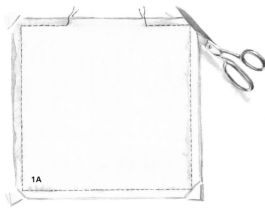

templates

The outlines shown below have all been reduced in size so they fit on these pages. To make them the correct size, enlarge them on a photocopier by the percentages given.

ETHEREAL THROW
(page 20) Enlarge by 175%

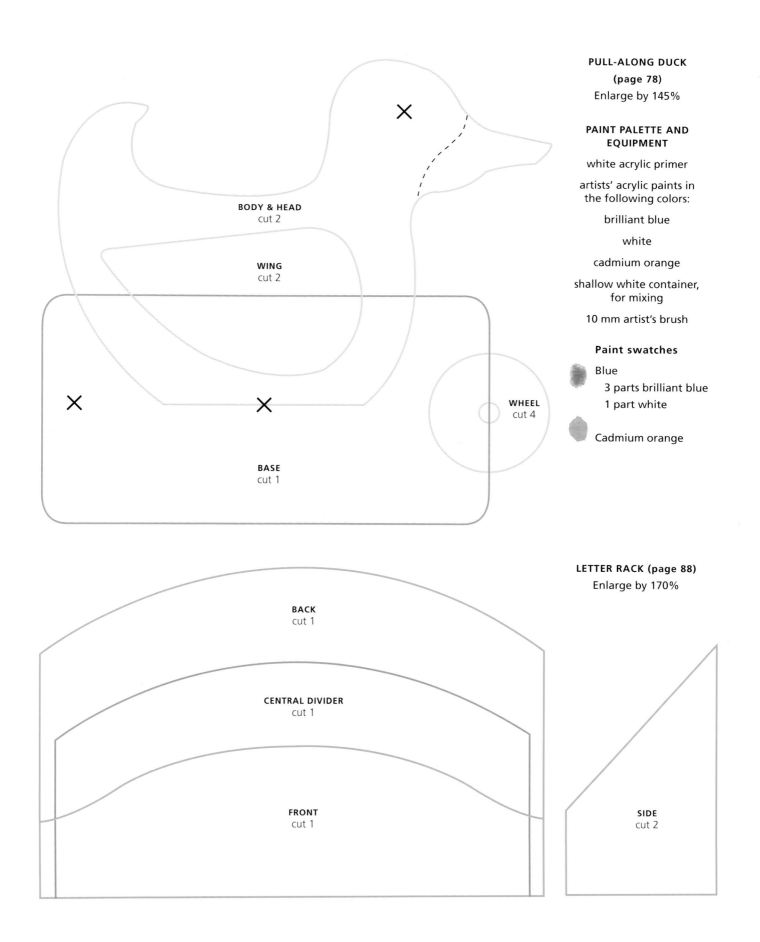

PULL-ALONG DUCK
(page 78)
Enlarge by 145%

PAINT PALETTE AND EQUIPMENT

white acrylic primer

artists' acrylic paints in
the following colors:

brilliant blue

white

cadmium orange

shallow white container,
for mixing

10 mm artist's brush

Paint swatches

Blue
3 parts brilliant blue
1 part white

Cadmium orange

BODY & HEAD
cut 2

WING
cut 2

WHEEL
cut 4

BASE
cut 1

LETTER RACK (page 88)
Enlarge by 170%

BACK
cut 1

CENTRAL DIVIDER
cut 1

FRONT
cut 1

SIDE
cut 2

sources

ABC CARPET & HOME
888 Broadway
New York, NY 10003
t. 212-473-3000
www.abccarpet.com
Large-scale home accessories store, specializing in carpets.

BED, BATH, & BEYOND
620 Avenue of the Americas
New York, NY 10011
t. 212-255-3550
www.bedbathandbeyond.com
Department stores with everything for the home.

BLANKS FABRICS
6709 Whitestone Road
Baltimore, MD 21207
t. 410-944-0040
www.blanksfab.com
Will track down those hard to find fabrics and textiles from around the world.

CALICO FABRIC SHOP
10 West Street
W. Hatfield, MA 01088–954
t. 413-247-9989
www.calicofabric.com
Largest quilt shop in central and western Massachusetts. Inventory includes all major fabric manufacturing companies. Online catalog available.

CATH KIDSTON
201 Mulberry Street
New York, NY 10012
t. 212-343-0223
www.cathkidston.com
Bright and fresh 1950s-inspired florals and accessories. Fabrics available.

CONSO PRODUCTS
P.O. Box 326
Union, SC 29379
t. 800-842-6676
www.conso.com
One of the largest distributors of decorative trims, cording, ropings, tassels, and fringes in various fibers.

COVINGTON CANDLE
976 Lexington Avenue
New York, NY 10021
t. 212-472-1131
Tapers in 30 colors and six sizes, which will fit perfectly into different holders and decors. Pillars are also available in a number of sizes to order.

CRATE & BARREL
646 N Michigan Avenue
Chicago, IL 60611
t. 312-787-5900
www.crateandbarrel.com
A wonderful source of good-value china, glass, and plastic containers. Locations nationwide. Mail order. Catalog.

FLORACRAFT
One Longfellow Place
P.O.Box 400
Ludington, MI 49431
t. 231-845-5127
www.floracraft.com
Distributors of wreath, topiary, and geometric forms made of Styrofoam, extruded foam, and straw; also available is a vast array of floral supplies and accessories.

FISKARS MANUFACTURING CORP.
P.O. Box 1727
Wausau, WI 54401
t. 715-842-2091
www.fiskars.com
Manufacturers of fine-quality scissors, snippers, paper edgers, and punchers, and the useful Craft-Snip, which can be used to cut a variety of heavy-duty materials. They also make excellent tools for gardening and floral work.

HANCOCK FABRICS
2605A West Main Street
Tupelo, MS 38801
t. 662-844-7368
www.hancockfabrics.com
Everything you need for projects involving sewing or fabrics, including adhesives.

HIGH COUNTRY FLORAL
P.O. Box 155
Carlton, WA 98814
t. 509-923-2646
f. 509-923-2037
www.highcountryfloral.com
Here you can find preserved and stem-dyed wreaths, garlands, and arches, as well as a wide selection of other preserved and dried flowers and leaves, herbs, and spices.

HOBBY LOBBY
t. 405-745-1100; ask for Customer Service
www.hobbylobby.com
Discount arts and crafts stores. Locations nationwide.

HOME DEPOT
t. 800-553-3199
www.homedepot.com
A wide selection of lumber, outdoor furniture, and plant material at discounted prices.

JO-ANN STORES, INC.
13323 Riverside Drive
Sherman Oaks, CA 91423-2508
t. 818-789-3167
t. 800-525-4951 for enquiries
www.joann.com
Craft supplies for all projects. Locations nationwide.

KATE'S PAPERIE
561 Broadway
New York, NY 10012
t. 212-941-9816
*Over 40,000 papers, many handmade,
plus cards, journals, and wrappings.*

LOOSE ENDS
P.O. Box 20310
Keizer, OR 97307
t. 503-390-7457
www.looseends.com
*A wide selection of natural-fiber papers,
ribbons, and botanicals, like seagrass,
raffia, dried fruits, and fungi.*

LOWE'S
www.lowes.com
Locations nationwide.
*Good source of garden accessories,
tools, and lumber.*

MAPLE RIDGE SUPPLY
9528 South Bolton Road
Posen, MI 49776
t. 517-356-4807
f. 517-354-6664
www.mapleridgesupply.com
*All sizes and shapes of metal wreath
forms.*

MELINAMADE FABRICS
420 Russell Street
Winters, CA 95694
t. 415-902-8460
www.melinamade.com
*Vintage inspired patterns on Barkcloth
cotton fabrics, wallpaper, and accessories.*

MICHAELS STORES, INC.
t. 800-MICHAELS for a store near you
www.michaels.com
*Specialty retailer of arts and crafts items.
Locations nationwide.*

M & J TRIM
1008 Sixth Avenue
New York, NY 10018
t. 212-842-5000
www.mjtrim.com
*Has an outstanding collection of
decoorative trims, cording, ropings,
tassels, and fringes in various fibers.*

M.P.R. ASSOCIATES, INC.
P.O. Box 7343
High Point, NC 27264
t. 800-454-3331
*This maker of nontraditional ribbons can
provide you with paper lace, corrugated
paper ribbons, wired and plain paper and
metallic ribbons, paper raffia, and paper
twist.*

A. C. MOORE
Styretowne Plaza
1069 Bloomfield Ave
Clifton, NJ 07012
t. 973-470-8885
www.acmoore.com
*Craft superstores. Over 70 stores
throughout Eastern US.*

PJ'S DECORATIVE FABRICS, INC.
511 West Broad Avenue
Albany, GA 31701
t. 229-439-7265
www.pjsfabrics.com
*Carries a large selection of home
decorating fabrics, trims, rugs, and more.*

POTTERY BARN
600 Broadway
New York, NY 10012
t. 212-219-2420
www.potterybarn.com
*Moderately priced garden furniture, a
variety of glassware, candlesticks, and
hurricane lamps. Locations nationwide.*

RAG SHOPS, INC.
t. 973-423-1303; ask for Customer Service
www.ragshop.com
*Offering a wide selection of value-priced
crafts, fabrics, floral, framing, and related
merchandise for the crafter and home sewer.*

ROBERT ALLEN
www.robertallendesign.com
*Quality decorative fabrics. Nationwide
storerooms.*

SCALAMANDRE FABRICS
222 East 59th Street
New York, NY 10022
t. 212-980-3888
www.scalamandre.com
Luxury textile manufacturer.

TINSEL TRADING CO.
47 West 38th Street
New York, NY 10018
t. 212-730-1030
www.tinseltrading.com
*Unique vintage-to-contemporary trims,
tassels, fringes, and cords.*

WAL-MART
t. 501-273-4000
www.walmart.com
Locations nationwide.

WAVERLY HOME STORE
For stores and stockists visit:
www.waverly.com
t. 800-527-2517

WOOD-N-CRAFTS, INC.
P.O. Box 140
Lakeview, MI 48850
t. 800-444-8075
f. 517-352-6792
www.wood-n-crafts.com
*A good source for unfinished wood, such
as candlesticks and candle cups, buttons,
stars, and hearts.*

index

picture credits

Key: ph=photographer, il=illustrator, a=above, b=below, r=right, l=left, c=center.

Endpapers Sandra Lane/cushions and throw from Cath Kidston; **1** ph Polly Wreford/Emma Greenhill's London home; **2** ph Catherine Gratwicke/Martin Barrell & Amanda Sellers' home, owners of Maisonette, London; **3** ph Debi Treloar/the home of Patty Collister in London, owner of An Angel At My Table; **4** ph Sandra Lane/the home of Patty Collister in London, owner of An Angel At My Table-cushions and throws vintage Cath Kidston at An Angel At My Table; **5** ph Tom Leighton; **6l** ph Debi Treloar/the guesthouse of the interior designer & artist Philippe Guilmin, Brussels; **6c** ph Debi Treloar /author, stylist and "Caravan" (shop) owner Emily Chalmers and director Chris Richmond's home in London; **6r** ph Debi Treloar; **7l** ph Caroline Arber/designed and made by Jane Cassini and Ann Brownfield; **7c** ph Polly Wreford; **7r** ph Tom Leighton; **8l** ph Caroline Arber; **8c** ph Catherine Gratwicke/Caroline Zoob's workroom; **8r** ph David Loftus; **9l** ph Polly Wreford; **9c** ph Caroline Arber; **9r** ph Sandra Lane; **10** ph Polly Wreford/Ros Fairman's house in London; **11l** ph Caroline Arber/designed and made by Jane Cassini and Ann Brownfield; **11c** ph Polly Wreford/Emma Greenhill's London home; **11r** ph Polly Wreford /Adria Ellis' apartment in New York; **12a** both ph Debi Treloar/Mark and Sally of Baileys Home and Garden's house in Herefordshire; **12b** ph Polly Wreford/Mary Foley's house in Connecticut; **13** ph Catherine Gratwicke/Laura Stoddart's apartment in London; **14** ph Debi Treloar/Anna Massee of Het Grote Avontuur (The Great Adventure)'s home in Amsterdam; **15al** ph Debi Treloar/the home of Studio Aandacht, design by Ben Lambers; **15ar** ph Catherine Gratwicke/Lulu Guinness's home in London; **15b** ph Polly Wreford/Emma Greenhill's London home; **16a** ph Catherine Gratwicke/Francesca Mills' house in London-70s scarf cushions from Maisonette; **16b** ph Catherine Gratwicke/Lucy and Marc Salem's London home-striped chair by Lucy Salem; **17al** ph Sandra Lane/the home of Patty Collister in London, owner of An Angel At My Table-square cushions from An Angel At My Table, bag by Cath Kidston at An Angel At My Table; **17ac** ph Debi Treloar/designer Petra Boase & family's home in Norfolk; **17ar** ph Sandra Lane/Karen Nicol and Peter Clark's home in London-cushion made by Karen Nicol; **17b** ph Catherine Gratwicke/Lulu Guinness's home in London; **18a** ph Catherine Gratwicke/the home of Patty Collister in London, owner of An Angel At My Table; **18bl** ph Sandra Lane/cushions made by Karen Nicol; **18br** ph Catherine Gratwicke/vintage floral cushions with velvet flowers by Lucy Salem; **18–19** ph Debi Treloar/designer Susanne Rützou's home in Copenhagen; **19ac&bc** ph Debi Treloar/Debi Treloar's home in London; **19ar** ph Debi Treloar/the Chestnut Hill home of Pamela Falk; **19br** ph Caroline Arber/designed and made by Jane Cassini and Ann Brownfield; **20–21** ph Sandra Lane, il Lizzie Sanders/Karen Nicol and Peter Clark's home in London–cushions and throw by Karen Nicol; **22–23** ph Sandra Lane, il Lizzie Sanders/cushions by Lucinda Ganderton; **24** ph Debi Treloar; **25al** ph Catherine Gratwicke; **25ar** ph Polly Wreford/Karen Nicol and Peter Clark's home in London; **25c,cr&bl** ph Debi Treloar; **25br** Polly Wreford; **26al** ph Catherine Gratwicke; **26ac** ph Catherine Gratwicke/Lulu Guinness's home in London; **26ar** ph Caroline Arber/designed and made by Jane Cassini and Ann Brownfield; **26bl** ph Catherine Gratwicke; **26br** ph David Loftus; **27 main** ph Catherine Gratwicke/Lulu Guinness's home in London; **27 inset** ph Debi Treloar/designer Petra Boase & family's home in Norfolk; **28** ph Catherine Gratwicke/Claudia Bryant's house in London-apron made by Emily Medley; **29l** ph Catherine Gratwicke/Laura Stoddart's apartment in London; **29c** ph David Brittain; **29r** ph Debi Treloar/the guesthouse of the interior designer & artist Philippe Guilmin, Brussels; **30al** ph David Brittain/kitchen designed and supplied by Cunningham Furniture; **30ar** ph Debi Treloar/Annelie Bruijn's home in Amsterdam; **30b** ph Debi Treloar/Anna Massee of Het Grote Avontuur (The Great Adventure)'s home in Amsterdam; **31** ph Debi Treloar/Cristine Tholstrup Hermansen and Helge Drenck's house in Copenhagen; **32al** ph Christopher Drake/Enrica Stabile's house in Brunello; **32ar** ph Catherine Gratwicke/Rose Hammick's home in London; **32b** Rose Hammick's home in London; **33al&ac** ph Caroline Arber/designed and made by Jane Cassini and Ann Brownfield; **33ar** ph Catherine Gratwicke/pan holder made by Lattika Jain; **33cr** ph Debi Treloar; **33b** all ph David Loftus; **34–35** ph Catherine Gratwicke, il Lizzie Sanders/Claudia Bryant's house in London-apron made by Emily Medley; **36al** ph Catherine Gratwicke/felt place mats made by Sasha Gibb, egg-cosies made by Cecilie Telle; **36ac** Sandra Lane; **36ar** ph Polly Wreford; **36bl** ph Debi Treloar; **36br** ph Catherine Gratwicke; **37** ph Debi Treloar/designer Susanne Rützou's home in Copenhagen; **38al** ph Catherine Gratwicke/Lesley Dilcock's house in London; **38ar** ph Tom Leighton; **38b** ph Catherine Gratwicke/Martin Barrell & Amanda Sellers' home, owners of Maisonette, London; **39a** ph Catherine Gratwicke/Lulu Guinness's home in London; **39bl** ph Caroline Arber/designed and made by Jane Cassini and Ann Brownfield; **39bc&br** ph Sandra Lane; **40–41** ph James Merrell, il Helen Smythe; **42** ph Alan Williams/the Norfolk home of Geoff & Gilly Newberry of Bennison Fabrics – fabric on wall Bennison's Daisy Chain; **43l** ph Debi Treloar/designer Petra Boase & family's home in Norfolk; **43c** ph Debi Treloar; **43r** ph Polly Wreford; **44a** ph Catherine Gratwicke/Rose Hammick's home in London; **44b** ph Catherine Gratwicke/the home of Patty Collister in London, owner of An Angel At My Table-dressing table from An Angel At My Table, curtain from Lucy Salem; **45a** ph Debi Treloar/Mark and Sally of Baileys Home and Garden's house in Herefordshire; **45b** ph Debi Treloar/designer Petra Boase & family's home in Norfolk; **46–47** ph James Merrell, il Lizzie Sanders/voile from Osborne & Little, lining from Designers Guild; **48al** ph Sandra Lane/vintage throw courtesy of Karen Nicol; **48ar** ph Sandra Lane/pillowcase from J&M Davidson, lavender bag from Graham & Green; **48b** all ph Sandra Lane; **49al** ph Chris Everard/fashion designer Carla Saibene's home in Milan; **49ar** ph Debi Treloar/the Philadelphia home of Kristin Norris, creative director at Anthropologie and Trevor Lunn, digital designer; **49b** ph Catherine Gratwicke/Rose Hammick's home in London; **50al** ph Catherine Gratwicke/retro laundry bags from The Laundry; **50ac** ph Catherine Gratwicke; **50bl** ph Catherine Gratwicke/lavender bag from Susannah, retro bedlinen from the Laundry; **50bc** ph Catherine Gratwicke/patchwork bag made from antique quilts and ticking by Sue Holley of Susannah in

Bath; **50–51** ph Catherine Gratwicke/Lesley Dilcock's house in London; **51a** ph Caroline Arber/designed and made by Jane Cassini and Ann Brownfield; **51bl** ph Catherine Gratwicke; **51br** Rose Hammick's home in London–patchwork quilt by Emily Medley; **52–53** ph David Montgomery, il Lizzie Sanders/Blakes Lodging designed by Jeanie Blake www.picket.com/blakesBB/blakes.htm, throw by Jeanie Blake; **54a** all ph David Brittain; **54bl** ph Caroline Arber/designed and made by Jane Cassini and Ann Brownfield; **54br** ph Sandra Lane; **55a** ph Catherine Gratwicke/Lucy and Marc Salem; **55cl** ph Debi Treloar/designer Susanne Rützou's home in Copenhagen; **55cr** ph Catherine Gratwicke; **55bl** ph Debi Treloar/Anna Massee of Het Grote Avontuur (The Great Adventure)'s home in Amsterdam; **55br** ph Catherine Gratwicke/interior designer Sue West's house in Gloucestershire; **56–57** ph Sandra Lane, il Lizzie Sanders/cushions made by Karen Nicol; **58** ph Chris Everard/Lulu Guinness's home in London; **59l&r** ph Chris Everard; **59c** ph Catherine Gratwicke; **60al** ph Debi Treloar/designer Petra Boase & family's home in Norfolk; **60ar** ph Tom Leighton; **60b** ph Debi Treloar/the guesthouse of the interior designer & artist Philippe Guilmin, Brussels; **61 main** ph Tom Leighton; **61 inset** ph Caroline Arber/Hoggy & Mark Nicholl's home in Wiltshire; **62 main** ph Polly Wreford; **62 inset** ph Debi Treloar/the home of Patty Collister in London, owner of An Angel At My Table; **63bl** ph Debi Treloar; **63al** ph Catherine Gratwicke/Claudia Bryant's house in London-vintage fabric-lined towel from Lucy Salem; **63ar** ph Debi Treloar/the Chestnut Hill home of Pamela Falk; **63br** ph Catherine Gratwicke/Lucy and Marc Salem's London home; **64–65** ph Catherine Gratwicke, il Lizzie Sanders/designer Caroline Zoob's home in East Sussex-floral Dorothy bag made by Caroline Zoob; **66al** ph David Montgomery; **66ar,bl&br** ph Tom Leighton; **66cl&cr** ph Chris Everard; **67a&br** ph Christopher Drake/Enrica Stabile's houses in Le Thor, Provence & Brunello; **67bl** ph Debi Treloar/author, stylist and "Caravan" (shop) owner Emily Chalmers and director Chris Richmond's home in London; **68** ph Debi Treloar/Debi Treloar's home in London; **69l** ph Debi Treloar/owner of Crème de la Crème à la Edgar, Helle Høgsbro Krag's home in Copenhagen; **69c** ph Sandra Lane; **69r** ph Catherine Gratwicke/the home of Patty Collister in London, owner of An Angel At My Table- painting from An Angel At My Table; **70** both ph Debi Treloar/owner of Crème de la Crème à la Edgar, Helle Høgsbro Krag's home in Copenhagen; **71al** ph Christopher Drake/Marisa Cavalli's home in Milan; **71ar** ph Debi Treloar/Ben Johns & Deb Waterman Johns' house in Georgetown; **71br** ph Debi Treloar/Victoria Andreae's house in London; **72al** ph Debi Treloar/designer Petra Boase & family's home in Norfolk; **72ar** ph Sandra Lane/Sophie Eadie's family home in London-strawberry cushions from The Cross; **72br** ph Sandra Lane/the home of Patty Collister in London, owner of An Angel At My Table–bed and quilt from An Angel At My Table, pillowcase made by Lucinda Ganderton; **73 main** ph Sandra Lane/Sophie Eadie's family home in London; **73l** inset ph Caroline Arber/patchwork blanket by Olga Tyrwhitt; **73r** inset ph Debi Treloar/designer Petra Boase & family's home in Norfolk; **74–75** ph Catherine Gratwicke, il Lizzie Sanders/café curtain made from children's hankies by Lucinda Ganderton; **76al** ph Debi Treloar/Victoria Andreae's

house in London; **76ar** ph Debi Treloar/owner of Crème de la Crème à la Edgar, Helle Høgsbro Krag's home in Copenhagen; **76cl** ph Debi Treloar/Ben Johns & Deb Waterman Johns' house in Georgetown; **76cr** ph Debi Treloar; **76bl** ph Catherine Gratwicke/cushion made by Greta Zoob; **76br** ph Catherine Gratwicke; **77** ph Debi Treloar/Cristine Tholstrup Hermansen and Helge Drenck's house in Copenhagen; **78–79** ph David Montgomery, il Michael Hill; **80** ph Caroline Arber/designed by Jane Cassini and Ann Brownfield; **81l** ph Sandra Lane; **81c** ph Catherine Gratwicke/studio of Sasha Gibb, colorist, interior consultant and designer-covered chair, handwork and printed length by Sasha Gibb; **81r** ph Debi Treloar/Mark and Sally of Baileys Home and Garden's house in Herefordshire; **82a** ph Debi Treloar/owner of Crème de la Crème à la Edgar, Helle Høgsbro Krag's home in Copenhagen; **82b** ph Polly Wreford; **83a** ph Debi Treloar/Cristine Tholstrup Hermansen and Helge Drenck's house in Copenhagen; **83b** ph Debi Treloar/the guesthouse of the interior designer & artist Philippe Guilmin, Brussels; **84a** Adamczewski, Hélène Adamczewski's shop in Lewes-apron made by Lattika Jain; **84b** ph Catherine Gratwicke/the home of Patty Collister in London, owner of An Angel At My Table; **85al** ph Catherine Gratwicke; **85ac&ar** ph Caroline Arber/designed and made by Jane Cassini and Ann Brownfield; **85bl** ph Polly Wreford; **85bc&br** ph Catherine Gratwicke; **86al,ac&cl** ph Polly Wreford; **86bl** ph Sandra Lane; **86ar** ph Caroline Arber/designed and made by Jane Cassini and Ann Brownfield; **86br** ph Debi Treloar/Mark and Sally of Baileys Home and Garden's house in Herefordshire; **87** ph Caroline Arber/designed and made by Jane Cassini and Ann Brownfield; **88–89** ph David Montgomery, il Michael Hill; **90** ph Christopher Drake/Enrica Stabile's house, Le Thor, Provence; tablecloth, cushions & teacup, L'Utile e il Dilettevole; **91l** ph Christopher Drake/ iron bed, antique bedspread & cushions from L'Utile e il Dilettevole; **91c** ph Francesca Yorke; **91r** ph Catherine Gratwicke; **92al** ph Christopher Drake/Mr & Mrs Degrugillier, Le Mas de Flore, Antiquite et Creation, Lagnes, Isle sur Sorgue, Provence-garden table & chair from Le Mas de Flore, cushion from l'Utile e il Dilettevole; **92ar&b** ph Christopher Drake/designer Barbara Davis' own house in upstate New York; **93a** ph Christopher Drake/Enrica Stabile's house in Brunello; **93b** ph Christopher Drake/Guido & Marilea Somaré's house in Milan-garden chair, l'Utile e il Dilettevole; **94** ph Christopher Drake/La Bastide Rose, Nicole & Pierre Salinger's house, Le Thor, Provence- iron bed, garden chair, tin candlestick, cotton bag, antique bedspread & all cushions, L'Utile e il Dilettevole; **95al** ph Christopher Drake/Enrica Stabile's house in Provence; cushion & throw, L'Utile e il Dilettevole; **95ac** ph Sandra Lane/cushions and throw from Une Histoire Simple; **95ar** ph Catherine Gratwicke/peg bag made by Lattika Jain; **95b** Sandra Lane/cushions and throw from Cath Kidston; **96al,bl,cr&ar** all ph Francesca Yorke; **96cl** ph Marianne Majerus; **96br** ph Francesca Yorke/artist Marylin Phipps' house in Kent; **97a** ph Caroline Arber/designed and made by Jane Cassini and Ann Brownfield; **97bl&br** ph Christopher Drake; **98–99** ph Marianne Majerus, il Michael Hill/wire-work basket designer Jane Seabrook at The Chelsea Gardener.

business credits

ADAMCZEWSKI
88 High Street
Lewes
East Sussex BN7 1XN
t. +44 (0)1273 470105
adamczewski@onetel.net.uk
Fine houseware.
Page **84a**

AN ANGEL AT MY TABLE
116A Fortess Road
Tufnell Park
London NW5 2HL
t. +44 (0)20 7424 9777
f. +44 (0)20 7424 9666
www.angelatmytable.co.uk
Painted furniture and accessories.
Pages **3**, **4**, **17al**, **18a**, **44b**, **62inset**, **69r**,
72b, **84b**

**ANNA MASSEE OF HET GROTE
AVONTUUR**
Het Grote Avontuur
Haarlemmerstraat 25
1013 EJ Amsterdam
t. 020 6268597
www.hetgroteavontuur.nl
Pages **14**, **30b**, **55bl**

ANNELIE BRUIJN
t. +31 653 702869
annelie_bruijn@email.com
Page **30ar**

ANTHROPOLOGIE
t. +800 309 2500
www.anthropologie.com
Page **49ar**

BAILEYS HOME & GARDEN
The Engine Shed
Station Approach
Ross-on-Wye
Herefordshire HR9 7BW
t. +44 (0)1989 563015
f. +44 (0)1989 768172
www.baileyshomeandgarden.com
Pages **12al**, **12ar**, **45a**, **81r**, **86br**

BARBARA DAVIS
Designer
t. +1 607 264 3673
Pages **92al**, **92b**

BENNISON
16 Holbein Place
London SW1W 8NL
t. +44 (0)20 7730 8076
bennisonfabrics@btinternet.com
www.bennisonfabrics.com
Page **42**

BOIS-RENARD
t. +1 215 247 4777
Decorative home accessories.
Pages **19ar**, **63ar**

CARLA SAIBENE
Carla Saibene (shop)
via San Maurilio 20
Milano
Italy
t/f. +39 2 77 33 15 70
xaibsrl@yahoo.com
*Womenswear collection, accessories,
and antiques.*
Page **49al**

CAROLINE ZOOB
Shop A
33 Cliffe High Street
Lewes
East Sussex BN7 2AN
t. +44 (0)1273 476464 (shop & mail order)
www.carolinezoob.com
Hand-made collectables.
Pages **8c**, **64–65**

CECILIE TELLE
cecilietelle@hotmail.com
t. +44 (0)20 7272 1335
*Felted wool products for children & adults,
and for the kitchen.*
Page **36al**

CLAUDIA BRYANT
t. +44 (0)20 7602 2852
Pages **28**, **34**, **63al**

CRÈME DE LA CRÈME À LA EDGAR
Kompagnistræde 8,st
1208 Copenhagen K
t. +45 33361818
Pages **69l**, **70 both**, **76ar**, **82a**

CUNNINGHAM FURNITURE
t. +44 (0)20 8674 1743
Page **30al**

DEBI TRELOAR
www.debitreloar.com
Pages **19ac**, **19bc**, **68**

EMMA GREENHILL
egreenhill@freenet.co.uk
Pages **1**, **11c**, **15b**

EMILY CHALMERS
Author & stylist
emily@emilychalmers.com
Caravan (shop)
11 Lamb Street
Spitalfields
London E1 6EA
t. +44 (0)20 7247 6467
www.caravanstyle.com
Pages **6c**, **67bl**

EMILY MEDLEY
Designer
emilymedley@mac.com
Pages **28**, **34–35**, **51br**

ENRICA STABILE
L'Utile e il Dilettevole (shop)
Via Carlo Maria Maggi 6
20154 Milano
t. +39 0234 53 60 86
www.enricastabile.com
*Antiques dealer, interior decorator,
and photographic stylist.*
Pages **32al**, **67a**, **67br**, **90**,
91l, **93**, **94**, **95al**

FRANCESCA MILLS
Designer/stylist
t. +44 (0)20 7733 9193
f. +44 (0)20 7274 8861
Page **16a**

HOGGY'S ANTIQUES TOYS &
TEXTILES AT SHARLAND & LEWIS
52 Long Street
Tetbury
Gloucester GL8 8AQ
t. +44 (0)1666 500354
www.sharlandandlewis.com
Page **61 inset**

THE HOUSEMADE
Sue West
t/f. +44 (0)1453 757771
sue.west@btopenworld.com
Interior & product design
Page **55br**

JANE CASSINI
jane_vintagestyle@yahoo.com
Pages **7l,11l, 19br, 26ar, 33al, 33ac, 39bl,**
51a, 54bl, 80, 85ac, 85ar, 86ar, 87, 97a

KAREN NICOL EMBROIDERY
t. +44 (0)20 8979 4593
Pages **17ar, 18bl, 20–21, 25ar,**
48al, 56–57

LATTIKA JAIN
t. +44 (0)20 8682 3088
Freelance in textile design, fashion,
& knitwear.
Pages **33ar, 84a, 95ar**

LUCY SALEM
t. +44 (0)20 8563 2625
lucyandmarcsalem@hotmail.com
Makes and sources soft furnishings
and decorative items for the home.
Pages **16b, 18br, 44b, 55a, 63al, 63br**

LULU GUINNESS
3 Ellis Street
London SW1X 9AL
t. +44 (0)20 7823 4828
f. +44 (0)20 7823 4889
www.luluguinness.com
Pages **15ar, 17b, 26ac, 27 main, 39a, 58**

MAISONETTE
t. +44 (0)20 8964 8444
f. +44 (0)8964 8464
maisonette.uk@aol.com
www.maisonette.uk.com
Pages **2, 16a, 38b**

MARISA CAVALLI
via Solferino, 11
20121 Milano
Italy
t. +39 02 36 51 14 49
f. +39 02 29 00 18 60
marisacavalli@hotmail.com
Page **71al**

OLGA TYRWHITT
tyrwhitt@ntlworld.com
Textile artist, courses available.
Pages **73 inset left**

PETRA BOASE
www.petraboase.com
info@petraboase.com
Pages **17ac, 27 inset, 43l, 45b, 60al,**
72al, 73 inset right

PHILIPPE GUILMIN
Interior designer & artist
philippe.guilmin@skynet.be
Pages **6l, 29r, 60b, 83b**

RÜTZOU A/S
t. +45 35 24 06 16
f. +45 35 24 06 15
www.rutzou.com
cph@rutzou.com
Pages **18–19, 37, 55cl**

SASHA GIBB
t/f. +44 (0)1534 863211
home@sashagibb.co.uk
Interior and color consultant
Contemporary home furnishings designed
and made from vintage blankets
Pages **36al, 81c**

STUDIO AANDACHT
ben.lambers@studioaandacht.nl
www.studioaandacht.nl
Art direction and interior production.
Page **15al**

SUSANNAH
25 Broad Street
Bath BA1 5LW
Pages **50bl, 50bc**

THE CHELSEA GARDENER
125 Sydney Street
Kings Road
London SW3 6NR
t. +44 (0)20 7352 5656
f. +44 (0)20 7352 3301
www.chelseagardener.com
Pages **98–99**

acknowledgments

Although it is my name that appears on the title page, this book is very much a joint project with the editorial, creative and production teams at RP&S. I would like to thank everybody who has made it possible and especially Miriam for her editorial guidance, Anne-Marie for her art direction, Emily for once again selecting such interesting pictures, and Megan for putting them all together on the page.

Copyright information
(continued from page 4)
All projects have been previously published by Ryland, Peters & Small

Page 20 Ethereal Throw by Karen Nicol. Previously published in *Pillows & Throws* by Lucinda Ganderton, © 2003.

Page 22 Transfer Print Cushion by Lucinda Ganderton. Previously published in *Pillows & Throws* by Lucinda Ganderton, © 2003.

Page 34 Apron by Emily Medley. Previously published in *Vintage Fabric Style* by Lucinda Ganderton and Rose Hammick, © 2003.

Page 40 Heart of Fresh Roses by Paula Pryke. Previously published in *Wreaths & Garlands* by Paula Pryke, © 1998.

Page 46 Voile Bed Canopy by Katrin Cargill. Previously published in *Simple Beds* by Katrin Cargill, © 1998.

Page 52 Diamond Bedcover by Jeanie Blake. Previously published in *Pillows, & Throws* by Lucinda Ganderton, © 2003.

Page 56 Diamanté Cushion by Karen Nicol. Previously published in *Pillows & Throws* by Lucinda Ganderton, © 2003.

Page 64 Floral Dorothy Bag by Caroline Zoob. Previously published in *Pillows & Throws* by Lucinda Ganderton, © 2003.

Page 74 Handkerchief Curtain by Lucinda Ganderton. Previously published in *Vintage Fabric Style* by © Lucinda Ganderton and Rose Hammick, © 2003.

Page 78 Pull-along Duck by Stewart & Sally Walton. Previously published in *Painted Woodcraft* by Sally and Stewart Walton, © 1997.

Page 88 Letter Rack by Stewart & Sally Walton. Previously published in *Painted Woodcraft* by Sally and Stewart Walton, © 1997.

Page 98 Wirework Basket by Jane Seabrook. Previously published in *Containers* by George Carter, © 1997.